World Heritage and Tourism

This book provides a comprehensive discussion of the phenomenon of World Heritage tourism through a critical, global perspective that encompasses both supply and demand.

Individual chapters critically engage with four main topics crucial to this subject area. A chapter on visitors defines the World Heritage tourist segment, highlighting on-site behavior and visitor needs. Building on this, a marketing chapter questions the functionality of the World Heritage brand as a tourist attractor and instead argues that tourist growth is due to effective marketing following World Heritage inscription. The third chapter presents a holistic management framework centered on planning, place, and people, while the concluding chapter situates World Heritage tourism in a global context, discussing threats such as climate change. International case studies from a wide variety of both natural and cultural sites provide a representative discussion of the topic across varying geographical, political, and cultural contexts.

This will be of great interest to upper-level students, researchers, and academics in the fields of tourism, heritage studies, and geography, as well as practitioners in these fields who wish to better understand the crucial interplay of these areas.

Bailey Ashton Adie is a Research Fellow at Solent University in Southampton, UK. She has a Ph.D. in Management and Development of Cultural Heritage from IMT Lucca, Italy. She also has an MA in Cultural Heritage and International Development from the University of East Anglia, Norwich, UK. Her research focuses on World Heritage tourism in an international comparative context, sustainable heritage tourism for community development, tourism marketing and branding, second-home tourism and climate change, and film tourism.

Routledge Focus on Tourism and Hospitality

Routledge Focus on Tourism and Hospitality presents small books on big topics and how they intersect with the world of tourism and hospitality research. The idea is to fill the gap between journal article and book. This new short-form series offers both established and early career academics the flexibility to publish cutting-edge commentary on key areas of tourism and hospitality, topical issues, policy-focused research, analytical or theoretical innovations, a summary of the key players or short topics for specialized audiences in a succinct way.

World Heritage and Tourism
Marketing and Management
Bailey Ashton Adie

For more information about this series, please visit: www.routledge.com/tourism/series/FTH

World Heritage and Tourism
Marketing and Management

Bailey Ashton Adie

Routledge
Taylor & Francis Group

LONDON AND NEW YORK

First published 2019 by Routledge

2 Park Square, Milton Park, Abingdon, Oxon OX14 4RN

605 Third Avenue, New York, NY 10017

Routledge is an imprint of the Taylor & Francis Group, an informa business

First issued in paperback 2022

Publisher's Note

The publisher has gone to great lengths to ensure the quality of this reprint but points out that some imperfections in the original copies may be apparent.

British Library Cataloguing-in-Publication Data
A catalogue record for this book is available from the British Library

Library of Congress Cataloging-in-Publication Data
Names: Adie, Bailey Ashton author.
Title: World heritage and tourism : marketing and management / Bailey Ashton Adie.
Description: First edition. | New York : Routledge, 2019. | Series: Routledge focus on tourism and hospitality | Includes bibliographical references and index.
Identifiers: LCCN 2019011111 (print) | LCCN 2019020744 (ebook) | ISBN 9780429506659 (eBook) | ISBN 9781138583603 (Hardback : alk. paper)
Subjects: LCSH: Heritage tourism—Management. | Hospitality industry—Management.
Classification: LCC G156.5.H47 (ebook) | LCC G156.5.H47 A25 2019 (print) | DDC 910.68—dc23
LC record available at https://lccn.loc.gov/2019011111

ISBN: 978-1-138-58360-3 (hbk)
ISBN: 978-1-03-233839-2 (pbk)
DOI: 10.4324/9780429506659

Typeset in Times New Roman
by Apex CoVantage, LLC

For André, with all my love.

Contents

Figures

Boxed cases

Acknowledgments

This book has been front and center in many personal conversations, and I am sure that my friends and family will be glad to be done hearing about it. With that in mind, I want to first apologize to anyone who had to listen to me rant about the writing process during the course of this book. To begin, I need to thank Michael Hall, without whom this book, and my Ph.D., would not have been possible. A special thank you to coffee for more or less the same reasons. Thank you also to Carlotta, Lydia, and Emma from Routledge for making this a straightforward, relatively painless process.

I would like to thank Shaina, Brittany, and Rene for their constant support from across the ocean and Steve for his from Liverpool. I want to thank Ellena for distracting me when it was all too much. I would like to thank all my friends at the office for letting me ask them odd questions throughout the day and cheering me on. Thank you to my family for supporting me, even if most of you could never quite remember what my book was about. Thank you to my siblings, Courtney and Alex, for always calling, with all the best intentions, right when I was about to write something profound. Extra thanks need to go to my parents, Rich and Debbie, who talked me off the proverbial ledge more than once. Finally, I would like to thank my husband, André, who has been with me during this whole journey and who has provided unwavering support, even when he risked life and limb even speaking to me. I couldn't have done it without you.

Acronyms

HDI   Human Development Index
ICOMOS International Council on Monuments and Sites
IUCN   International Union for Conservation of Nature
NGO   Non-governmental organization
UNESCO United Nations Educational, Scientific, and Cultural Organization

1 Introduction

An introduction to World Heritage

The United Nations Educational, Scientific, and Cultural Organization, or as it is more commonly known, UNESCO, was created in November 1945, only two months following the end of the Second World War, with a mandate "to promote peace and security through the application of education, science and culture to international understanding and human welfare" (Valderrama, 1995, p. 25). One of the key motivating events for the development of the World Heritage Convention occurred in 1959, following a request for assistance from the Egyptian and Sudanese governments. Due to the construction of the Aswan Dam, a collection of ancient Egyptian monuments, including the Abu Simbel temples, were under threat from flooding by the Nile. An international coalition was developed, which worked collaboratively to remove the monuments and reconstruct them out of harm's way. Further international collaborations were initiated in response to several other major threats, notably the massive flooding in Venice in 1966 (Singh, 2011). It was these events that led to the drafting of the UNESCO Convention Concerning the Protection of the World Cultural and Natural Heritage on the 16th of November 1972.

The USA was the first to ratify the convention in 1973, followed by Algeria, Australia, Bulgaria, Democratic Republic of the Congo, Egypt, Iraq, Niger, Nigeria, and Sudan in 1974, and, after the collection of a sufficient number of signatories, the convention went into effect in 1975. This outlined a program for the creation of a global heritage regime, which effectively laid the groundwork for the eventual creation of the World Heritage List, onto which the first 12 sites were inscribed in 1978. As a result of the broad acceptance of the World Heritage Convention, there has been exponential growth both in the number of States Parties that are signatories and sites on the World Heritage List itself. At the time of writing, the total number of States Parties that have ratified the convention totals 193, with the most recent signatories having been South Sudan and Timor-Leste in 2016. These were the first new ratifications of the convention since the Bahamas in 2014. Of those 193 States Parties, 167 have listed sites, and as of 2018, there are 1,092 sites on the list, of which 845 are cultural, 209 natural, and 38 mixed (UNESCO, n.d.-c).

While the overall goal of the World Heritage Convention is the protection of sites of Outstanding Universal Value, UNESCO has also identified World Heritage mission priorities:

- Encourage countries to sign the World Heritage Convention and to ensure the protection of their natural and cultural heritage;
- Encourage States Parties to the Convention to nominate sites within their national territory for inclusion on the World Heritage List;
- Encourage States Parties to establish management plans and set up reporting systems on the state of conservation of their World Heritage sites;
- Help States Parties safeguard World Heritage properties by providing technical assistance and professional training;
- Provide emergency assistance for World Heritage sites in immediate danger;
- Support States Parties' public awareness-building activities for World Heritage conservation;
- Encourage participation of the local population in the preservation of their cultural and natural heritage;
- Encourage international cooperation in the conservation of our world's cultural and natural heritage.

(UNESCO, 2008, p. 3)

These stress the responsibility that States Parties have for the protection and conservation of their own heritage, placing state sovereignty at the forefront. In fact, while UNESCO functions as a monitoring body, they have little power to enforce conformity to World Heritage norms.

The process of World Heritage inscription

Although the World Heritage List is protected under the World Heritage Convention and organized by the World Heritage Committee, UNESCO is not actually responsible for the selection of nominated sites. Instead, it is the responsibility of the respective States Parties to place sites on their tentative lists, which is the only way in which a site can officially be nominated to the World Heritage List (UNESCO, 2017). While the tentative list can technically include as many sites as a State Party chooses, new regulations have gone into effect from 1 February 2018 that limit nominations to 1 per year with a maximum of 35 to be considered per annual committee meeting. In order to be successfully nominated, sites must include a Statement of Outstanding Universal Value, the key component to being a World Heritage site. UNESCO defines Outstanding Universal Value as "cultural and/or natural significance which is so exceptional as to transcend national boundaries and to be of common importance for present and future generations of all humanity" (UNESCO, 2017, p. 19).

In order to be considered of Outstanding Universal Value, sites must fulfill at least one of the following criteria:

I   Represent a masterpiece of human creative genius;

II Exhibit an important interchange of human values, over a span of time or within a cultural area of the world, on developments in architecture or technology, monumental arts, town-planning, or landscape design;

III Bear a unique or at least exceptional testimony to a cultural tradition or to a civilization which is living or which has disappeared;

IV Be an outstanding example of a type of building, architectural or technological ensemble or landscape which illustrates (a) significant stage(s) in human history;

V   Be an outstanding example of a traditional human settlement, land use, or sea use, which is representative of a culture (or cultures), or human interaction with the environment especially when it has become vulnerable under the impact of irreversible change;

VI Be directly or tangibly associated with events or living traditions, with ideas, or with beliefs, with artistic and literary works of outstanding universal significance. (The Committee considers that this criterion should preferably be used in conjunction with other criteria) ;

VII Contain superlative natural phenomena or areas of exceptional natural beauty and aesthetic importance;

VIII Be outstanding examples representing major stages of earth's history, including the record of life, significant on-going geological processes in the development of landforms, or significant geomorphic or physiographic features;

IX Be outstanding examples representing significant on-going ecological and biological processes in the evolution and development of terrestrial, fresh water, coastal, and marine ecosystems and communities of plants and animals;

X   Contain the most important and significant natural habitats for in-situ conservation of biological diversity, including those containing threatened species of Outstanding Universal Value from the point of view of science or conservation.

(UNESCO, 2017, pp. 25–26)

Until 2005, these criteria were divided, with criteria I through VI being strictly for cultural sites, and VII to X were used to describe natural sites. They have since been combined to create a comprehensive list of ten criteria.

In addition to these criteria, all sites are required to satisfy three additional requirements: integrity, protection, and management. Integrity is defined in the UNESCO Operational Guidelines (2017, p. 27) as "a measure of the wholeness and intactness of the natural and/or cultural heritage and its attributes." In order to evaluate a site's integrity, the following must be considered:

a) Includes all elements necessary to express its Outstanding Universal Value;
b) Is of adequate size to ensure the complete representation of the features and processes which convey the property's significance;
c) Suffers from adverse effects of development and/or neglect.

(UNESCO, 2017, pp. 27–28)

As has been mentioned, in addition to integrity, sites are also required to have effective protection measures in place in order to preserve the site's Outstanding Universal Value. These include on-site protections and sufficient buffer zones, as well as appropriate legislative systems. The final condition for listing, which must be fulfilled by all nominated sites, is the provision of an adequate management plan or system for the site. However, "management systems may vary according to different cultural perspectives, the resources available and other factors. They may incorporate traditional practices, existing urban or regional planning instruments, and other planning control mechanisms, both formal and informal" (UNESCO, 2017, p. 31). Therefore, this aspect can be flexible in acknowledgment of the diversity of contexts within which sites are located.

Additionally, mixed and purely cultural sites, those whose statements of Outstanding Universal Value includes any criteria from I to VI, must also illustrate that their sites are authentic. Authenticity in this context is defined by the Nara Document on Authenticity (ICOMOS, 1994), which stresses respect toward the plurality of cultural practice inherent in a global system. According to the Operational Guidelines (UNESCO, 2017, p. 27), site qualities that can be put forward for consideration in the assessment of a site's level of authenticity include

- form and design;
- materials and substance;
- use and function;
- traditions, techniques, and management systems;
- location and setting;
- language and other forms of intangible heritage;
- spirit and feeling; and
- other internal and external factors.

As can be seen, the concept of authenticity is purposefully vague in order to ensure inclusivity and prevent cultural bias. However, assertions of authenticity must still have evidentiary support, from "physical, written, oral, and figurative sources" (UNESCO, 2017, p. 27), which need to be included in the application materials.

Only upon satisfaction of the requirements for integrity, protection, management, and, in the case of sites with a cultural component, authenticity can a site be submitted to the relevant State Party's tentative list. Currently, 183 States Parties have submitted tentative lists to the World Heritage Committee, with 177 active lists containing 1,710 tentative World Heritage sites available for consideration for inscription. Once on a tentative list, the properties are evaluated by two independent expert advisory bodies: the International Union for Conservation of Nature (IUCN) and the International Council on Monuments and Sites (ICOMOS). Cultural heritage listings are evaluated by ICOMOS, and the IUCN assesses natural sites. In the case of mixed sites, both bodies are responsible for submitting evaluations to the World Heritage Committee. Based on the findings from these evaluations, the IUCN, ICOMOS, or both for mixed sites can make three potential recommendations:

a) Properties which are recommended for inscription without reservation;
b) Properties which are not recommended for inscription;
c) Nominations which are recommended for referral or deferral.
(UNESCO, 2017, p. 40)

While the first two recommendations are fairly self-explanatory, it is perhaps necessary to clarify the third. Referral and deferral both postpone a final committee decision, albeit for slightly different reasons. Referral requires a State Party to submit further data to the committee before a decision can be made. Deferral, instead, is more involved, necessitating a "more in depth assessment or study, or a substantial revision by the State Party," with the entire nomination requiring a second round of evaluations by the relevant advisory bodies. In both cases, the nomination will be reevaluated by the World Heritage Committee in the hopes of attaining a successful inscription.

Inequalities of the World Heritage List

While World Heritage sites are located across the globe, there are several visible disparities within the List itself. The first, and most obvious, is that related to the regional distribution of sites. World Heritage sites are organized in regional groups – namely, Africa, Arab States, Asia and the Pacific, Europe and North America, and Latin America and the Caribbean. However, these regions do not necessarily correspond to the geographical locations of the sites. For example, the Arab States region, and not the African one, includes North African States Parties. Another example is the existence of a Europe and North American region, given the physical distance between the two. Additionally, Israel, geographically in Asia, is included in this region, while Mexico, which is in North America, is in the Latin America and the Caribbean group. As observed in Figure 1.1, Europe and North America dominate the list with 514 total sites followed by Asia and the Pacific with 258. This regional dominance exhibits itself clearly in the top-ten States Parties with the most listed sites. Of these,

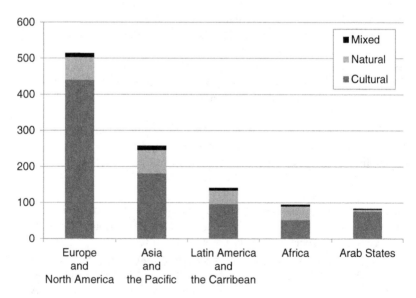

Figure 1.1 Regional distribution of World Heritage sites

seven are found in Europe and North America (Italy, Spain, France, Germany, the UK, Russia, and the USA) with two in Asia and the Pacific (China and India), and one in Latin America and the Caribbean (Mexico). This disconnect between the phrasing of the World Heritage Convention in reference to the universal value of World Heritage sites and the predominance of one specific region in terms of actual listings has been found to be a significant problem. An attempt to redress this issue is visible in the implementation of the Global Strategy in 1994. The strategy was the resulting policy following an ICOMOS study undertaken between 1987 and 1993. "[This study] revealed that Europe, historic towns and religious monuments, Christianity, historical periods and 'elitist' architecture (in relation to vernacular) were all over-represented on the World Heritage List; whereas all living cultures, and especially 'traditional cultures,' were underrepresented" (UNESCO, 2008, p. 15). In order to redress this inequality, the strategy not only broadened the definition of what could be considered heritage but also encourages new signatories and new nominations from underrepresented States Parties. Additionally, it prioritizes listings from States Parties that have few or no listed sites over those parties that are already very well represented (Musitelli, 2002). Regardless, the list is still dominated by the Europe and North America regional group.

While Europe and North America's total presence on the List is less than half at 47%, Asia and the Pacific, which comes in second in terms of representation, contains only 23.6% of all listed sites. Furthermore, although Europe and North America have marginally fewer listed natural heritage sites than Asia and the Pacific, they dominate the list in terms of cultural heritage, with over 52% of all listed cultural heritage sites found in their territory. Moreover, of the 684 sites added to the World Heritage List after 1994, 308 (45%) are located in Europe and North America, and 177 (25.9%) are found in Asia and the Pacific. Thus an argument could be made that, in terms of actual listings, the Global Strategy is an ineffective program, as the largest number of sites inscribed since the beginning of the program are still located in Europe and North America, and the list is dominated by two regions, accounting for 70.9% of all listings that have occurred since the Global Strategy's inception.

Ashworth and van der Aa (2006, p. 149) observed that "the harder UNESCO has tried to redress these 'imbalances,' however, the more they have grown, at least in terms of spatial distribution." This is supported by Elliott and Schmutz (2016) who found that inscription of African sites was falling behind the rest of the world. In fact, Strasser (2002) made this precise point when he noted little change in terms of the dominance of cultural sites in comparison with natural ones, as well as the general composition of the

World Heritage List. While UNESCO has attempted to develop a framework of unity in diversity for its sites,

> there are civilizations for which the notion of heritage is not the same as the notion of monuments. The efforts made by the world heritage organs to integrate this dimension of the problem . . . remain too timid to absorb the contradiction between universality and diversity.
>
> (Musitelli, 2002, p. 330)

Ergo, although the Global Strategy attempts to be inclusive, without a firm understanding of all potential conceptualizations of heritage, the current system will inevitably exclude certain cultures that do not conform to Western ideologies related to heritage.

While the geographical distribution of sites has been previously discussed (see Strasser, 2002), there exists a less evident inequality within the World Heritage List. Specifically, there is a huge difference in terms of listing on different levels of development, as per the Human Development Index (HDI). There is a striking imbalance between those countries found at the bottom of the HDI rankings when compared with those at the top. The top 20 account for 23% of the total list, while the bottom 20 contain only 3% of all World Heritage sites. This disproportionate share of sites is of particular interest given that the origins of the World Heritage Convention are tied to periods of crisis in countries that were ill equipped to handle the potential damages to their heritage. In fact, UNESCO (2008, p. 10) states that "a key benefit of ratification, particularly for developing countries, is access to the World Heritage Fund." While the World Heritage Fund will be discussed further in the chapter on holistic World Heritage management, it is interesting to note that those who have the strongest economic need for assistance in regard to conservation have so few sites on the list when compared with those in a better economic situation. This may also be an indication of the cost of both developing site nominations and those associated with the management of sites after listing.

Bertacchini and Saccone (2012) proposed another theory to explain the dominance of certain countries on the World Heritage List. In their research, they discovered two specific factors, political and economic, that impacted the inscription of a site. The first of these related to a country's position on the World Heritage Committee wherein those on the Committee were significantly more likely to see their nominated sites listed, especially those designated as cultural sites. However, "the longer a country stays in the World Heritage System, the lower the probability of having a site included in the List," which was explained by general trend related to the largest number of sites usually being nominated shortly after signing the convention (Bertacchini & Saccone, 2012, p. 345). They also determined that "economic power is relevant for the capacity of countries to propose heritage sites for the List but not for the probability of having sites inscribed" (Bertacchini & Saccone, 2012, p. 348). Thus, political and economic power, generally, have a significant impact on a State Party's ability to put forth a successful site nomination, which has negative implications for those same countries that the Global Strategy seeks to assist.

Frey et al. (2013) drew similar conclusions in their study where they observed that, in general, countries that have higher levels of economic development have more World Heritage sites. This contradicts Bertacchini and Saccone's (2012) statement that economic power does not assist in the actual listing of a site. However, this economic power becomes irrelevant according to their data related to the number of sites in connection with a rotating member position on the UN Security Council. Based on these results, they also determined "that the power of a country on the World Heritage Committee is exerted more by its influence on international bodies instead of its level of economic development" (Frey et al., 2013, p. 15). Thus a country needs either a high level of economic development or political power in order to succeed in its World Heritage nominations, but it does not need to possess both as Bertacchini and Saccone (2012) suggested. Furthermore, Frey et al. (2013, p. 18) emphasize that the fact that the List is politically relevant asserts its significance, especially as "politicians, public officials, and interest groups in the various countries find it desirable to try to influence the selections on the List." This then supports the necessity of the Global Strategy, as the subjectivity of the World Heritage List can be called into question.

World Heritage and tourism: an introduction

Tourism and World Heritage have become inextricably linked in the years since the creation of the World Heritage List. However, the World Heritage Convention, as has been mentioned, was originally designed as a means to protect and conserve heritage deemed to be of global importance. This is still its primary function, and tourism is not even mentioned in main text of the current Operational Guidelines (UNESCO, 2017). Interestingly, though, it does appear in the annex, which details the general content of the questionnaire used for periodic reporting, a post-listing activity. According to Annex 7, the portion of the questionnaire that deals explicitly with the "state of conservation" of the site contains a specific segment in which States Parties must report "on tourism activities and visitor management at the property" (UNESCO, 2017, p. 118). Therefore, while not clearly visible in the Operational Guidelines, the presence of tourism within the periodic reporting questionnaire illustrates an awareness of the fact that the vast majority of World Heritage sites are not only accessible but also host at least a moderate number of tourists. This is further emphasized by UNESCO (2008, p. 10), which states that "the inscription of a site on the World Heritage List brings an increase in public awareness of the site and of its outstanding values, thus also increasing the tourist activities at the site." In acknowledgment of this relationship between tourism and World Heritage, UNESCO created the World Heritage and Sustainable Tourism Program. This program's mission is to "facilitate the management and development of sustainable tourism at World Heritage properties through fostering increased awareness, capacity, and balanced participation of all stakeholders in order to protect the properties and their Outstanding Universal Value" (UNESCO, n.d.-b).

This program was the direct result of Decision 34 COM 5F.2 (UNESCO, 2010), which stressed the importance of tourism for World Heritage as a simultaneous risk and resource for sites. Furthermore, this text, in Attachment A, emphasizes the fact that the World Heritage brand functions well as a tourist attractor, particularly to less famous sites, and can provide economic advantages to the World Heritage sites as well as the surrounding areas (UNESCO, 2010). Perhaps, then, it is unsurprising that States Parties place so much emphasis on the tourism impacts of World Heritage. They share the belief that the presence of World Heritage sites will increase tourist numbers, thus providing an infusion of, preferably, foreign currency into the economy (e.g. Patuelli et al., 2013; Su & Lin, 2014; Yang et al., 2010). This conviction is best exemplified by the statement made by Giovanni Puglisi, the former president of the Italian National Commission for UNESCO, who said, "It has been proven that inscription to the World Heritage list increases tourism flows by between 20 and 30%" (Berni, author's translation, 2005, p. 11). However, as will be seen in this book, this appears to be a misplaced belief, thus potentially exacerbating inequalities on the ground in an attempt to inscribe a site above all else.

Outline of the book

In order to provide a holistic overview of the current relationship between tourism and World Heritage, this monograph is composed of three core chapters presenting an analysis of both the supply and demand aspects of tourism at World Heritage sites, followed by a chapter highlighting current issues facing World Heritage and potential future developments in the World Heritage tourism nexus. The demand is addressed first in order to provide a tourist-centered narrative to the work. While this initial chapter begins with a presentation of more general tourist typologies, it swiftly moves into a discussion of who exactly can be considered a World Heritage tourist, including the findings from previous research involving visitor segmentation studies at World Heritage sites and recent work explicitly identifying a World Heritage tourism subsegment. Following this presentation of a World Heritage tourist typology, the focus of the chapter shifts to World Heritage visitor activities while actually on-site. Additionally, it is also essential to understand the requirements of these World Heritage tourists during their visits. This includes general needs as well as those that are more specialized in relation to site type – i.e., authenticity at cultural sites. The chapter ends with a disclaimer that even with a perfect understanding of the World Heritage tourist, events outside of a site's control can lead to an unavoidable negative experience for the visitor.

Following this identification of who the tourists that visit World Heritage sites are and identifying their on-site behavior and needs, the second chapter presents an overview of marketing for tourism at World Heritage sites, with a special emphasis on the World Heritage brand. The chapter begins with a brief, general discussion of tourism marketing and branding in order to provide a lens through which to view the World Heritage brand. It then moves into a critical discussion of the World Heritage brand through an introduction to previous research on the impact of the brand on visitation as well as that analyzing visitor awareness of the brand. While this included studies that support and those that refute UNESCO's claims that the World Heritage brand attracts tourists, there are significantly more studies that find that it is not an effective brand. Therefore, it is determined that World Heritage may have significantly less power as a tourism brand than generally thought, which poses potential problems for sites relying on tourism increases merely as a result of listing. However, it would appear that active marketing campaigns, regardless of the World Heritage brand's power, may be sufficient to attract new visitors, especially as they tend to be aimed at more diverse markets.

Regardless of whether or not World Heritage inscription increases tourist visitation, any World Heritage site that intends to promote tourism activity on-site requires sufficient tourism planning and management frameworks in place. With this in mind, the final core chapter presents a holistic management strategy, which highlights the intersection of three key themes: Planning, Place, and People. The Planning theme focuses on governance and policy frameworks within the World Heritage system that interact with the other two themes at varying levels, but predominantly in relation to the local. This theme emphasizes the structure of the World Heritage management system but not the specificities. Those fall under the theme of Place, as they are predominantly context-driven requirements within a specific environment. The Place segment, then, discusses the development of sustainable tourism management on-site in relation to challenges such as conservation in the face of tourism and overtourism. Furthermore, there is a specific focus on World Heritage and tourism management in the context of international development, as there is a noted push to inscribe sites from less developed countries, specifically in the hope of raising their development levels. However, this can cause problems when tourism brings more problems than benefits. This leads to the final theme, People, which focuses on the need to center the local community at the heart of the World Heritage system, and the problems that arise when this group is sidelined from various aspects of the World Heritage management process.

This book concludes by situating World Heritage tourism into a broader global context. It begins with a presentation of the threats currently facing World Heritage sites around the world – i.e., terrorism, vandalism, damage from overtourism. However, while these are potentially major threats to a large number of sites, only global climate change is acknowledged as placing every single World Heritage site at risk. Although recognized as a global threat, this chapter specifically discusses how this will directly impact on World Heritage sites and tourism, and what potential actions may need to be taken to minimize climate change's impact on sites. Given how vulnerable these threats make World Heritage, the chapter then moves into a discussion on the inadequacies of the World Heritage system in its current form, particularly in regard to conservation issues. Finally, the chapter throws into the spotlight some of the problems associated with the linking of World Heritage and tourism, and the suitability of tourism at World Heritage sites, particularly given the stated goals of the World Heritage Convention, is questioned.

2 Visitors to World Heritage sites

Introduction

In order to fully discuss the interaction between tourism and World Heritage, it is necessary to first understand the core market, the tourists, and this is often precisely what is missing from the World Heritage tourism literature. Tourism is a demand-driven service industry, which simply means that tourists are the epicenter and driver behind its activity. As World Heritage tourism can be understood as a niche market within tourism, the chapter commences with a general discussion of tourist typologies, beginning with broad types before narrowing into more heritage-specific ones. This then shifts into the identification of who precisely is a World Heritage tourist, drawing on both nonsegmentation-specific studies as well as recent work specifically identifying a World Heritage tourist group. Once World Heritage tourists are identified, their on-site activities are presented as well as a brief discussion around the depth to which they tend to interact with the sites. Finally, the chapter discusses the variety of needs a tourist may have while visiting a World Heritage site. These range from the mundane, such as toilet facilities, to the more complex, like perceptions of authenticity. While all of this data can potentially allow sites to provide a better visitor experience, the chapter ends with a word of warning, as there are many aspects of tourism outside of a site's control which may result in a negative experience, regardless of the technical visit being "ideal."

Tourist typologies

In one of the earliest segmentation studies, Cohen (1972) proposed that there were four typologies of tourists: the organized mass tourist, the individual mass tourist, the explorer, and the drifter. The organized mass tourist is the least adventurous of the four, preferring the familiar and comfortable, and traveling on fully planned group excursions. This desire for the familiar is shared with the individual mass tourist, but this group tends to prefer to travel independently, albeit with a predominantly preplanned itinerary. Cohen (1972) referred to these two groups as institutionalized tourists, as they are very dependent upon the tourist infrastructure. In contrast, both the explorer and the drifter are classified as noninstitutionalized tourists, as they tend to have little, if any, interaction with this same infrastructure. These groups search for the unfamiliar, though the explorers still desire a level of comfort in relation to their travel amenities. The drifter, however, seeks total immersion and avoids all aspects of traditional tourism. Thus, these four groups are separated, in part, by their participation in the tourism structure as it existed in the 1960s and '70s.

Given the proximity in terms of publication period, it is unsurprising that Cohen's types are similar in nature to those proposed by Plog (1974). His classification is presented as a normal distribution along a spectrum from psychocentric to allocentric, with most tourists falling in the mid-centric group. For reference, psychocentric tourists are similar to Cohen's (1972) organized mass tourists in their strong preference for familiarity. In contrast, the fully allocentric are closer to the drifters found in Cohen's typology, as they prefer to avoid tourist activities and eschew the familiar (Plog, 1974). Upon Plog (2001) revisiting his tourist typology, he found that, overall, it was still valid. The only alteration proposed was in relation to nomenclature, changing the psychocentrics to dependables and the allocentrics to venturers. He also reinforced his conclusion that the majority of tourists would still fall in the middle of these two groups, as only "about 2 ½ percent of the population can be classified as Dependables and slightly over 4 percent as Venturers" (Plog, 2001, p. 17). However, he did acknowledge that there was some blurring due to travel developments that had occurred in the 30 years since his original paper had been published, particularly venturers engaging in travel types similarly to dependables and dependables traveling much more in general (Plog, 2001).

Both of these typologies focus on segmenting tourists as a whole, but, when discussing World Heritage tourism, it becomes necessary to use more specific niche tourism typologies, more precisely those segmenting cultural heritage and nature-based tourists. According to McKercher (2002, p. 30), a cultural tourist is

> someone who visits, or intends to visit, a cultural tourism attraction, art gallery, museum or historic site, attend a performance or festival, or participate in a wide range of other activities at any time during their trip, regardless of their main reason for traveling.

This is a fairly broad description, which covers a myriad of diverse albeit interconnected tourism activities. In an attempt to apply the previous general tourism typologies with the more specific niche of cultural heritage tourism, Chandler and Costello (2002) undertook a study that tested Plog's typologies at US cultural heritage sites located in the eastern hills of Tennessee. They found that, as Plog had stated, the vast majority were centrics, comprising 83.2% of all respondents. Only 9.5% were noted as being dependables and 7.3% as venturers (Chandler & Costello, 2002). This further agrees with Plog's (2001) research, wherein it was noted that falling into either of the two extremes of the normal distribution was very rare. However, while this typology can be applied to a cultural heritage destination, it still falls short of being a true cultural tourist typology.

In an attempt to further differentiate this tourist type, Stebbins (1996) identified three distinct groups on the basis of their investment in cultural tourism as a hobby-based pursuit. Those who occasionally participate in cultural activities but do not actively pursue them are referred to as cultural dabblers. This group is distinct from cultural tourists, who are subdivided into two separate segments. General cultural tourists, the most common type, enjoy visiting varied places and indulging in multiple cultural activities, during which they engage in general knowledge collection. Specialized cultural tourists instead tend to focus on one specific location or locations in order to gain a deeper cultural understanding of their contexts. However, these are much less common than the previously mentioned general cultural tourists.

This typology is still quite broad in terms of segmentation specificities, which led McKercher (2002) to develop a typology that fused depth of experience on-site with the level of importance that cultural tourism played in their destination choice. This resulted in five specific subtypes of cultural tourists: purposeful, sightseeing, casual, incidental, and serendipitous. The purposeful cultural tourist is who may come to mind when considering the niche cultural tourism market as a whole. They are the ones who chose to visit a destination based on its cultural attributes and search for profundity in their cultural interactions. Sightseeing, casual, and incidental tourists all exhibit lower levels of engagement with the destination, seeking what McKercher (2002, p. 32) refers to as "a more shallow, entertainment-oriented experience." These three groups are differentiated by the importance with which a destination's cultural offering played in their decision to visit. The sightseeing group placed the most weight on culture, followed by casual cultural tourists. Incidental cultural tourists may best be described as the opportunist visiting a famous cultural/heritage site because "it's there." Interestingly, while purposeful, sightseeing, casual, and incidental tourists are noted as encompassing the bulk of cultural tourists, "the serendipitous cultural tourist represents an anomaly. Cultural tourism factors play little or no role in the decisions to visit a destination for this person, yet, when participating in cultural tourism, he or she has a deep experience" (McKercher, 2002, p. 33). When this typology was applied to visitors to Hong Kong, sightseeing cultural tourists comprised slightly less than one-third of the total sample. Casual and incidental tourists were each approximately one-quarter, with purposeful and serendipitous cultural tourists being the two smallest groups. This model was tested a second time by McKercher and du Cros (2003), again in Hong Kong, and the distributions were fairly similar, though with slightly more purposeful cultural tourists and fewer serendipitous ones.

Similarly to McKercher (2002), whose typology is, in part, based on motivation to visit cultural aspects of destinations, Poria et al. (2003) proposed a typology that segmented visitors based on motivation, awareness, and personal connection to a heritage site, which in this study was the Wailing Wall in Israel. Their findings revealed four distinct groups. The first is similar to McKercher's (2002) incidental tourist in that the group members were unaware of the site's heritage. The second group was conscious of the heritage but wasn't motivated by it. In comparison, the third group was motivated by the Wailing Wall's heritage but had no personal heritage-based connection to the site. Thus the fourth, and final, group is unique in that it not only exhibited heritage-based motivation but also felt personally tied to the heritage. Poria et al. (2003, p. 249) stress that "heritage tourism stems from the relationship between the supply and the demand. It is not so much the attributes themselves, but the perceptions of them which is critical." As can be seen, this typology differs from those previously discussed due to its emphasis on tourists' connection to a heritage site in relation to their own personal heritage, which adds an emotional element unseen in previous segmentations.

While there are multiple segmentation studies focusing on cultural heritage tourists, visitors to natural sites are very difficult to segment, in part due to the extremely diverse definition of "nature tourism" (Kruger et al., 2017). Therefore, it is unsurprising that there are few segmentation studies specifically focusing on natural heritage tourists. Those that do segment visitors may choose to focus on tourist activity while in the boundaries of the protected area (Hvenegaard, 2002). This was the segmentation method used in Butzmann and Job (2017) who clustered visitors to Berchtesgaden National Park in Germany into six subtypes. The special nature experience (ecotourists) group was driven by knowledge acquisition, and thus it is unsurprising that a larger proportion of these tourists stopped by the visitor center or took part in guided experiences. In contrast, two hedonistic groups were identified: one with low and the other with high activity. These two segments were focused on shopping and taking walks as opposed to fully engaging in the natural tourism experience. The nature experience (hiker) group would fall somewhere in between these two groups. They are interested in sightseeing, hiking, and taking pictures. Unsurprisingly, this is similar to the nature experience (sports) group, whose members are, in addition to the previously mentioned activities, also involved in outdoor sports (i.e. mountain biking, mountain climbing). They are distinct from the mountaineering subtype, as the mountaineers' activity in the park is dominated by mountain climbing, often independently, and overnight stays to facilitate this climbing. Distance can also play a factor in segmentation, as was observed in Kruger et al. (2017). Their study identified three specific sub-groups of nature tourists among visitors to Kruger National Park in South Africa. The study used local names for trees to identify the groups, but they can be generally described as follows: locals, non-local domestic visitors, and international tourists. Both of the domestic groups spent approximately a week in the park, but the non-local visitors spent significantly more time than both of the other domestic visitors and the international tourists. The international visitors were predominantly return visitors who, in contrast to the domestic market, were unwilling to pay more to see what are termed the "Big Five" (African elephant, black rhinoceros, Cape buffalo, African lion, African leopard). As can be seen, segmentation can be deemed important, as it can sometimes illustrate potential problems with park management and marketing, particularly when these systems are based on general assumptions and not data. A similar contradictory finding was seen in Blamey and Braithwaite (1997), who used social values to segment ecotourists to natural parks in Australia. They found that one group, the Ideological Greens, were more geared toward environmental protection then the other three identified segments, but, interestingly, they also were the least likely to support entry fees to support the park's management (Blamey & Braithwaite, 1997). Based on general assumptions, this group should have been willing to pay more in order to assist in the protection of the site, but the data exhibited that this assumption, in this instance, would have been incorrect.

As has been seen, segmentation can greatly assist in the prevention of potential problems associated with incorrect assumptions about visitor behavior or needs. Thus it is unsurprising that tourist segmentation is important for marketers and destination managers alike, as "it can aid planning and lead to increased sales, lower costs and higher profitability" (Morgan & Pritchard, 2000, p. 151). This is especially relevant in relation to tourism destinations, as they need to provide a product that is distinct from their competitors in order "to attract industry and commerce and sustain the economic and social development of their inhabitants" (Baker & Cameron, 2008, p. 94). Moreover, these distinct products have to attract a required number of consumers in order to be deemed successful, and segmentation assists in this process. In fact, "one of the problems in marketing culture to tourists is that destinations often try and market their culture in general, offering a wide range of products, when many 'cultural tourists' are interested in much more specific experiences" (OECD, 2009, p. 56). A similar assumption could be made regarding the importance of differentiation in relation to marketing natural heritage. Thus tourist segmentation provides destinations with important information necessary to ensure that they are not simply attracting tourists but that they are actually reaching their core market.

World Heritage tourists

The importance of segmentation studies has been stressed in the previous section, and, while typologies appear to be more common in discussions of cultural heritage tourism, it is crucial to keep both natural and cultural heritage tourist types in mind when discussing World Heritage visitors. Given the wide array of segmentation studies, it is surprising that these same typologies have rarely been used in previous research focusing on World Heritage visitation, and those that have been undertaken have tended to apply McKercher's (2002). For example, Alazaizeh et al. (2016a) segmented visitors to Petra in Jordan wherein they found, similarly to McKercher (2002), that most tourists had superficial experiences on-site. However, a little less than three-quarters of all surveyed visitors fell into the sightseeing cultural tourist group, which is almost double that observed in McKercher (2002) and McKercher and du Cros (2003). The rest of the visitors to Petra were predominantly purposive cultural tourists with very few casual and incidental visitors and almost no serendipitous ones. Thus it would appear that visitors to Petra, overall, are strongly motivated by the site's cultural aspects, which is unsurprising given the site is far from the Jordanian capital of Amman, requiring in-country transport. In comparison, when segmenting visitors to Macao, Vong (2016) noted that the casual tourist group, which is a combination of McKercher's (2002) casual and incidental cultural tourists, was the largest group of cultural tourists in Macao. This can, again, perhaps be attributed to distance wherein visitors to Macao have easy access to the World Heritage site, as it is located in the city center.

Another motivation-driven segmentation that has been suggested relates to the concept of the World Heritage tourist as a collector, wherein the World Heritage List can be viewed as, and in certain cases has been treated as, a "collectable set" (Buckley, 2002, 2004). Previous research by Timothy (1998) identified three types of tourist collectors among the general tourist population. The first prioritize distinction, wanting to have traveled somewhere unique, and the second visit to improve their "numbers" in order to be able to quantify how extensively they have traveled. The final group "collect places for the sole purpose of impressing others by their choice of destinations" (Timothy, 1998, p. 127). When applying this categorization to World Heritage tourists, an assumption could be made that most collectors would fall within the second or third groups. Those in the second group would emphasize visiting as many World Heritage sites as possible, and visitors in the third group would be most likely to visit those destinations that are not only World Heritage sites but also have significant name recognition – i.e., the Taj Mahal in India, the Great Wall of China, Machu Picchu in Peru. As was observed in Baral et al.'s (2017) study on Sagarmatha National Park, visitors to World Heritage sites may also be focused on unique experiences that are impossible to replicate outside of these locations, resulting in a blending of the first and third type of tourist collectors.

To compound the complicated nature of collecting World Heritage sites, the list currently has more than 1,000 sites and is only expanding. Given the enormity of this, King and Prideaux (2010, p. 239) suggested that tourists may instead focus on collecting themed portions of the list – i.e., "all the World Heritage Areas in [the visitor's] own country, all the natural World Heritage Areas in Africa, or cultural areas in Europe containing Roman ruins." Thematic collection could potentially be helpful for site marketers, as Buckley (2004) suggested that site collection may cause an increase in visitation. However, this cannot be guaranteed, as World Heritage collection is most likely practiced only a by a very small subset of the tourist population, as was seen in King and Prideaux (2010). Furthermore, King and Prideaux (2010) found that their specialized World Heritage collectors could not be segmented based on demographics, which leads to the conclusion that World Heritage collectors select their thematic segments based on their own, individual curiosity. Therefore, when marketing to this group, only motivations can be considered (King & Prideaux, 2010).

While the previous studies have segmented on a variety of factors, with demographics generally having been used as subtype descriptors, there are several studies that do type cultural and natural heritage tourists specifically on their demographic characteristics. Cultural heritage tourists have generally been described as middle class (Huh et al., 2006; Kerstetter et al., 2001; Light & Prentice, 1994), well educated (Huh et al., 2006; Kerstetter et al., 2001; Light & Prentice, 1994; Nguyen & Cheung, 2014), and fairly evenly distributed between male and female respondents (Huh et al., 2006; Nguyen & Cheung, 2014; Richards, 2007). Most authors have also found that cultural heritage tourists are middle aged (Chandler & Costello, 2002; Huh et al., 2006; Kerstetter et al., 2001; Light & Prentice, 1994), but this has been contradicted by Richard's (2007) findings showing a trend toward a majority of visitors being in their 20s. In terms of tourists' country of residence, only Huh et al. (2006) and Nguyen and Cheung (2014) high-lighted this aspect, with almost exclusively domestic visitation in the case of Huh et al. and predominantly foreign in Nguyen and Cheung. Nature-based tourists exhibit similar trends to cultural heritage tourists. They tend to be middle aged (Meric & Hunt, 1998; Stoddard et al., 2008; Weaver & Lawton, 2002), middle class (Marques et al., 2010; Meric & Hunt, 1998; Stoddard et al., 2008; Weaver & Lawton, 2002), and highly educated (Marques et al., 2010; Meric & Hunt, 1998; Stoddard et al., 2008; Weaver & Lawton, 2002). However, unlike at cultural heritage sites, female visitors were more dominant in several studies (Marques et al., 2010; Weaver & Lawton, 2002), although Stoddard et al. (2008) note that in their sample, men are more likely to prefer nature-based activities over women. Thus, if applied to World Heritage sites, this would imply that World Heritage tourists are also middle class, middle aged, and well educated, with other demographic factors being contextually variable.

This demographic type is assumed when applying general or broad niche tourism typologies to World Heritage visitors, and, until recently, this assumption has been untested. This is not to say that demographic data has been ignored in past studies of World Heritage visitation but that it was not, generally, the research focus. The exception is Remoaldo et al. (2014), who were investigating the impact of gender on visiting a World Heritage site. While their results show no gender-specific interactions, they did have a higher number of female respondents, which is consistent with the reported demographics in several other World Heritage studies (Hazen, 2009; King & Halpenny, 2014; King & Prideaux, 2010; Piggott-McKellar & McNamara, 2017; Remoaldo et al., 2014). This is not universal, though, as was seen in Palau-Saumell et al. (2012), where gender was evenly split and Su and Wall (2016) who had more male than female respondents. In many studies, World Heritage visitors were predominantly young adults (i.e., King & Halpenny, 2014; Palau-Saumell et al., 2012; Piggott-McKellar & McNamara, 2017; Remoaldo et al., 2014; Su & Wall, 2016), yet, as with gender, there are contrasting examples. The largest proportion of World Heritage visitors to natural sites in the USA were middle aged (Hazen, 2009), and, at one natural site in Australia, there was no age-based majority at all (McGuiness et al.'s, 2017). The majority of studies also found that, as with the general cultural and natural heritage tourist types, World Heritage visitors tend to be more highly educated (King & Prideaux, 2010; Palau-Saumell et al., 2012; Piggott-McKellar & McNamara, 2017; Su & Wall, 2016).

In addition to gender, age, and education levels, tourists' country of residence has also been presented in several previous works. While it may be presumed that there would be parity between domestic and foreign tourists or even a preponderance of foreign visitors given the emphasis on World

Heritage sites' global value, not all World Heritage sites have large numbers of foreign visitors. For example, domestic travel would appear to be more common in the USA, as more than 80% of Hazen's (2009) sample of natural World Heritage site visitors in the USA were domestic. However, the dominance of domestic visitors is not found only in the USA. A similar trend in domestic visitation can be seen also in Ghana, where domestic visitors are the majority at Cape Coast and Elmina Castle, which are part of the Forts and Castles, Volta, Greater Accra, and Central and Western Regions World Heritage site (Reed, 2015). In Australia, domestic visitors were the overwhelming majority within McGuiness et al.'s (2017) sample from the Shark Bay World Heritage Area. A large number of domestic visitors was also observed at the Great Barrier Reef World Heritage Area by Piggott-McKellar and McNamara (2017). In contrast to these studies, King and Prideaux (2010) noted a higher proportion of international visitors to natural World Heritage sites in Australia. Therefore, World Heritage visitation may well follow the trends within the general natural and cultural heritage demographic identifiers with the dominance of domestic or international visitors being context specific.

Although the previous studies do take demographics into account in their research, there has been only one study to date that specifically focuses on identifying a demographically distinct group that could be defined as World Heritage tourists (Adie & Hall, 2017). Adie and Hall (2017) analyzed the data from visitor surveys at three geographically and thematically diverse World Heritage sites in order to understand visitor population trends at these sites. One of these findings relates to the ordinary residence of the World Heritage tourists, wherein Adie and Hall (2017) indicated that this residence did not exhibit any commonalities across their three case studies. For example, in their work, Independence Hall has a large proportion of domestic visitation, which can perhaps be tied to the importance of the site to the American historical narrative, as well as to general American identity. In contrast, visitors to Volubilis in Morocco were predominantly foreign. Additionally, Europeans were the largest subset within the foreign tourist grouping. Adie and Hall (2017, p. 78) suggested that this "could indicate that World Heritage is particularly attractive to Europeans" in part due to the European context of the convention.

Residence was not the only demographic factor that did not exhibit any cross-site trends in Adie and Hall (2017). They also indicated that there was no pattern in relation to age or income distribution. There were, however, several noted similarities across all three sites. Interestingly, gender was evenly distributed in their sample, similarly to the work of Palau-Saumell et al. (2012), which contradicts most previous World Heritage studies. Additionally, their findings indicate that World Heritage tourists are more likely to be employed or self-employed, traveling in groups of two to five people, and highly educated. The education aspect specifically confirms previous studies, both general and World Heritage specific. However, regardless of the educational similarities, the highlighted differences "would appear to separate the World Heritage visitor from the average heritage tourist whose identity is based in part on being middle class and middle aged" (Adie & Hall, 2017, p. 78). Therefore, using established segmentations designed for the more generalized nature-based and heritage tourism segments could potentially be problematic, as it makes demographic assumptions, which, as shown by Adie and Hall (2017), are not necessarily supported.

World Heritage visitor behavior

While the World Heritage tourist is a newly defined subtype of heritage tourists, there does exist a small body of literature that directly addresses what visitors to World Heritage destinations tend to do while on-site. One of the most common identified activities on-site is sightseeing and/or taking pictures of the location (Alazaizeh et al., 2016a; Hazen, 2009; Lenaertes, 2016; McGuiness et al., 2017; Su & Wall, 2016). One example is found in Hazen's (2009, p. 172) study, wherein almost 90% of visitors to the observed US natural sites stated that they planned to engage in sightseeing and appreciating the view. Unsurprisingly, these same visitors placed significant importance on the physical attributes of the natural sites and approximately one-quarter highlighted the strength of the sites' aesthetic aspects, which emphasizes the significance of these attributes for World Heritage visitors. These activities are further stressed in Box 2.1, which details on-site behavior of visitors to Yellowstone National Park. The importance of the site's aesthetics specifically for sightseeing and photography harken back to Urry's (2002) tourist gaze, wherein the World Heritage visitors are consuming the sign-posted landscape, based in part on preconceived notions of a destination that may be at least partly based on marketing efforts by the site or State Party in which it is located, which will be discussed in the following chapter.

Box 2.1   Visitor activity at Yellowstone National Park, USA

The World Heritage visitor on-site activities described in this chapter are clearly visible in the visitor population at Yellowstone National Park. Yellowstone is a large biosphere and natural World Heritage site located in the USA, predominantly in the northwest corner of the state of Wyoming, with the rest of the park resting at the borders of Montana and Idaho. Yellowstone National Park was established in

1872, making it the first national park in the world and predating the National Park Service by 44 years. As a result of its importance, in 1978, Yellowstone was one of the first sites inscribed on the World Heritage List. It was listed under all natural criteria, VII, VIII, IX, and X, for its "scenic treasures," important representation of geological history, and unique flora and fauna (UNESCO, n.d.-d). While people have been visiting Yellowstone since its establishment as a national park, access to the park became easier after the construction of a railroad link in 1883, and numerous hotels were built following its designation as a national park. However, in terms of volume, visitation really took off after the conclusion of the Second World War, with one million visitors arriving in 1948. Today, more than four million people visit the park every year, with the majority of all visits occurring between May and September (National Park Service, n.d.).

Based on a visitor survey undertaken by the National Park Service (2017) in 2016, it is clear that sightseeing is one of the key motivations for visiting, with 96% of all respondents indicating that "viewing natural scenery" was of high importance (National Park Service, 2017, p. 72). Unsurprisingly, then, it was also observed that photography was considered an important resource by approximately two-thirds of all respondents. Furthermore, most respondents indicated that Old Faithful geyser was an important resource for visitation, which, combined with the previous points, indicates that the majority of summer visitors to the site may have shallow experiences focused on a small number of key points of interest in the park. This is further supported by the fact that hiking was only deemed to be highly important by 44% of respondents, while 36% indicated it was of little to no importance for their visit (National Park Service, 2017, p. 169). Winter visitors are slightly more active, but more due to necessity as roads are generally closed to outside traffic during the winter months. Winter visitors may tour the park by cross-country skiing, snowshoeing, snowmobiling, and/or taking a snow coach tour, with the final two motorized options being the most popular (Freimund et al., 2009). However, even though winter conditions require a slightly more adventurous approach to park visitation, according to Freimund et al. (2009), the main focus of most visits is still sightseeing, albeit with a particular emphasis on observing the local bison population as opposed to the site's geologic attributes. Overall, it can be seen that visitation to Yellowstone is centered on visual consumption of the site, which is similar to the findings of other studies on visitor activities at World Heritage sites.

These imagined heritage landscapes are visible in both travel photography and popular representations of sites, either in film, on television, or through other multi-media images. For example, when someone says the words "Taj Mahal," a certain image is conjured in a person's mind: pristine white domes, curated gardens surrounding ornate water features, and long, empty pathways. This is the Taj Mahal of postcards and table books. The reality is slightly different. The fountains and domes are there, but it is not a private experience. There are crowds of people from all over the world on the walkways, and the silent awe presented in the photographs is replaced with a low hum of people talking, punctuated by the occasional yell of children. The emphasis on the idealized photographed image is visible in the results of the work of Cutler et al. (2015). Acknowledging the important link between tourism and photography, Cutler et al. (2015) undertook a study that included a visual analysis of tourist photography at Machu Pichu in Peru. Based on their findings, tourists preferred to capture images of an untouched site, void of other tourists or tourist infrastructure.

At some World Heritage sites, most notably natural ones that cover large swathes of ground, visitors may only be interested in shallow experiences focused on enjoying being in the area and seeing the "top spots," as was observed at one part of the Shark Bay World Heritage Area (McGuiness et al., 2017). For these visitors, it can be supposed that ease of access and protection of the aesthetic aspects of the site would be very important, emphasizing the need to take accessibility into account when discussing demand-side requirements. Boyd and Timothy (2006, p. 57) made a similar observation when they noted that, "for many international visitors, while [World Heritage sites] are viewed as attractions that may invoke feelings of awe, they probably do not invoke feelings of personal attachment." This in turn leads visitors to only spend a brief period on-site, often little more than a couple of hours (Boyd & Timothy, 2006). Thus it may be assumed that for a significant proportion of visitors to World Heritage sites, the emphasis will be on maximization of time, including all of the site's "hits" in as efficient a manner as possible.

While sightseeing is the most common activity undertaken by visitors to World Heritage sites, there are a myriad of others that can be enjoyed, dependent on the site type, location, and possible amenities. For example, tourists to the Temple of Heaven World Heritage site were interested in both the intangible and tangible cultural attributes of the site, with knowledge acquisition being a strong motivating factor for their visit (Su & Wall, 2016). This is to be expected, as the site is listed under cultural criteria. However, it is incorrect to assume that tourists only engage with World Heritage–specific aspects while on-site. An excellent representation of this is found in Hazen's (2009) research on visitors to natural World Heritage sites in the USA. While 53% of respondents planned on hiking around the site, 52% also indicated that they wanted to "visit historic sites," and 15% were going to engage in "prayer/reflection/contemplation" (Hazen, 2009, p. 172). Both of these activities are markedly cultural in nature, highlighting the often significantly complex visitor behaviors at World Heritage sites.

World Heritage tourist needs

Given the variety of World Heritage sites, not just in terms of type (i.e., natural, cultural, mixed) but also theme, location, size, and accessibility, it is unsurprising that World Heritage visitors would have a multitude of different needs. That being said, there are, of course, certain universal requirements for any tourist activity. For example, suitable transport both around and to and from the site is essential in order to ensure accessibility (Lenaertes, 2016). While accessibility can be an issue for all tourists dependent on the site type and location, there is an additional issue of accessibility for disabled visitors, which receives relatively little attention in the tourism literature (Yau et al., 2004). According to Chikuta et al. (2019), people with disabilities have a preference for natural areas, making them a particularly relevant group for natural World Heritage sites. However, when focused on accessibility, the application has to be holistic and include assistance for various types of disabilities, particularly focusing on the specific disabled market for the park (Chikuta et al., 2019). These alterations to assist with ease of access would be doubly beneficial given the aging populations in many countries, as these groups may also need access to sites improved, particularly in relation to mobility. A word of caution, however, should be added to these recommendations, particularly in relation to mobility. Transport on-site may not always be suitable, particularly at natural sites with fragile ecosystems. For example, at Phong Nha-Ke Bang National Park in Vietnam, visitation of in-park caves is highly promoted, but as some of the caves are quite difficult to access, tourist transport has been provided, which threatens the park merely through its existence (Lien, 2016).

Accessibility is also an issue when it comes to public toilet facilities, where there should be a disabled toilet available for use on-site. It needs to be stated, though, that the presence of public restrooms on-site or site adjacent are a necessity for tourism activity of any kind. Additionally, those that exist should be hygienic in order to ensure a positive experience. However, the essentiality of toilets is often neglected in the tourism literature. The omission of this aspect of tourism is particularly glaring, as the necessity of toilets is highly important, given that complaints regarding the lack or unsuitability of toilet facilities can negatively impact a tourist's visit, as was observed by Lenaertes (2016). Toilet facilities have come to the forefront in media discussions of US national parks in 2019 in light of the US government shutdown. During this event, government employees at the parks took a leave of absence, resulting in a serious degradation of visitor facilities. At Yosemite National Park, a natural World Heritage site, certain parts of the park were closed to visitors due to the shutdown. *The Guardian* (2019) reported that visitation had been spurred in part by the closure, as the shutdown resulted in the noncollection of entry fees to the parks. However, this also caused heavy strain on, most notably, the on-site toilet facilities, with many being closed due to the shutdown or already filled to capacity. This event illustrates exactly how important practical tourism infrastructure is not only to the tourist experience but also in the maintenance of site as a whole.

While the previous discussion around tourist infrastructure is related to more general requirements at all tourism destinations, World Heritage sites have certain specific obligations, notably around education. This responsibility is derived from Article 27 of the World Heritage Convention, which states that "the States Parties to this Convention shall endeavor by all appropriate means, and in particular by educational and information programs, to strengthen appreciation and respect by their peoples of the cultural and natural heritage" (UNESCO, 1972, p. 13). However, there is not always sufficient information available for visitors, as was observed by Crawford (2015). In her sample of visitors to Giants Causeway World Heritage site, a little under two-thirds of respondents felt that there was not enough on-site information and indicated that they would benefit from the addition of guided tours and/or individuals on the grounds who could answer questions. This need for information during a site visit, as well as the desire for proper tour guides, was echoed in Lenaertes (2016) and Salazar (2015). Therefore, the availability of educational materials is not only an on-site requirement as per the terms of the Convention but also an essential requirement for a satisfactory visitor experience. There is a danger, though, in providing extensive information at certain sites, as visitors expect equality of site interpretation, regardless of how developed the nation in which the site is situated (Shackley, 2006). This could potentially disadvantage less developed sites that, although they have a significant amount of information about the site, may not have the financial means to provide the same in-depth or guide-delivered experience.

In addition to physical infrastructure and education-based needs, World Heritage tourists also have certain intangible visitation requirements. For example, according to Esparon et al., (2015, p. 707), "visitors are seeking inspiring experiences which connect them in a personal way with special places, people, and cultures." Therefore, it is unsurprising that novelty would be identified as a factor when choosing to visit a World

Heritage site. At the Great Barrier Reef, the majority of surveyed visitors were motivated by a desire "to discover new places and things" (Piggott-McKellar & McNamara, 2017, p. 406). A similar trend was noted at the Singapore Botanic Gardens where "novel experience" became a more important push factor for visitors after the site was placed on the World Heritage List (Lee et al., 2018). In certain situations, visitors who seek novelty can, when their need for a unique experience is satisfied, provide more positive evaluations of other aspects of their visit. This was observed among visitors to Sagarmatha National Park in Nepal, wherein those who felt that their experience couldn't be replicated elsewhere had a more positive view of the site's Outstanding Universal Value (Baral et al., 2017). Thus, particularly given the emphasis on Outstanding Universal Value of each individual site as promoted by the Convention, a unique experience, if only in terms of the actual site's content, would be an expected component of a World Heritage site visit and therefore has been defined as a tourist need in this work.

Authenticity is a similarly abstract concept and yet deemed essential not only for listing but also for visitors. It needs to be stated that authenticity can include many things, including natural attributes. For example, environmental values were very important to visitors to the Great Barrier Reef World Heritage who identified a "clear ocean, healthy coral reefs, healthy reef fish and lack of rubbish" as key needs (Esparon et al., 2015, p. 719). In Kim et al.'s (2018) research undertaken at two Korean cultural World Heritage sites, which is, perhaps, a more traditional setting to discuss the need for authenticity, a stronger perception of authenticity resulted in a higher willingness to pay, which illustrates the potential economic power of authenticity. However, certain demographic variables may need to be taken into account, particularly given the specificities of the World Heritage visitor. According to the findings of Baral et al. (2017), higher levels of education resulted in lower levels of perceived authenticity, which can be particularly problematic at World Heritage sites given the fact that tourists to these sites generally are also more educated. Additionally, the perception of authenticity can be impacted by tangential activities on-site. For example, tourists to Chichen Itza, Mexico, found souvenir vendors on-site to be a nuisance, which, in combination with the often-dubious origin of the souvenirs on offer, may impact upon the perceived authenticity of the visitor experience (Milman, 2015). The absence of this activity, in contrast, can leave visitors with positive memories of their visit, as was seen in Luang Prabang, where tourists highlighted that one of the reasons that their visit to the site met or exceeded their expectations was due to the "friendly" local population "who did not hassle tourists" (Lenaertes, 2016, p. 65).

Unsurprisingly, it should be kept in mind that often a tourist's experience on-site is affected by factors outside of a site manager's control. For example, Cutler et al. (2015) noted that there was a marked difference between visitors to Machu Pichu, with those who had arrived via hiking the Inca Trail having more emotional ties to the site than the day visitors who were more focused on education. Additionally, anti-social behavior by other tourists has also been identified by some visitors as a negative aspect of site visitation. For instance, tourists at Luang Prabang highlighted inappropriate dress as a problem (Lenaertes, 2016). Dress codes are important at many sites, particularly in countries where there are cultural mores attached to certain types of clothing and a variety of religious sites. Recent problems have arisen across the globe related to issues with the dress of visitors, but it is often assumed in the media that these issues are part of local populations clashing with tourists. As can be seen, however, certain tourists are also bothered by the perceived disrespectful behavior of their fellow visitors. However, past experiences with World Heritage sites can have positive impacts on visitor perceptions of site attributes, notably Outstanding Universal Value, as was seen in the study by Baral et al. (2017). The caveat, then, is that even when tourists' needs are fulfilled, there is no guarantee that their visit will have met their expectations.

Conclusion

The significance of understanding the World Heritage market segment cannot be understated, particularly given the importance of marketing in relation to World Heritage tourism. However, to date, there has been little engagement with the demand-specific side of the field, which has led to many assumptions about World Heritage and tourism, as will be seen in the subsequent chapters. This chapter, though, has illustrated that World Heritage tourists do exhibit differences from the more general natural and cultural heritage tourist typologies. Therefore, marketing specifically designed for these broader groups may be missing a substantial part of the demographic. While identification of World Heritage tourists has implications for marketing, knowing what these tourists do on-site as well as what they need during their visit is essential to good management of World Heritage properties if the goal at these sites is the promotion of tourism. As has been noted, many tourists have shallow experiences and are highly interested in photography and viewing the landscape, with more in-depth and knowledge gathering experiences being more rare. This would appear to indicate that tourists may spend less time at a World Heritage site, particularly if they are only interested in "capturing" a few sites. However, regardless of the length of time spent on-site, all tourists need sufficient toilet facilities and accessible sites, where it doesn't harm the site itself. While these needs would be considered "universal," others are more specific to a tourist's personal expectations from a site – i.e., more information on-site, authenticity, and novelty. Finally, as was stressed in the introduction, even when tourist types are fully understood and their needs and desires met, they may still have unsatisfactory experiences due to actions completely outside of a site's control.

3 Marketing World Heritage for tourism

Introduction

While the previous chapter focused specifically on the demand-side of World Heritage tourism, marketing provides the platform for supply and demand to interact. In order to better understand World Heritage marketing practices, the chapter begins with a general presentation of tourism marketing, with an emphasis on branding and the various ways in which consumers can interact with a brand. This sets the stage for a critical discussion of the World Heritage brand, which is often promoted as a strong tourist attractor regardless of a lack of consensus on this assertion in the literature. While the examination of the World Heritage brand in this chapter presents both positive and negative views of its impact on visitation, the resulting discussion takes the position expressed by the author previously (Adie et al., 2018) – namely, that the brand functions as a placebo. Thus there is a recommendation to tread cautiously when relying on World Heritage brand-driven tourism increases, particularly when motivated by an expectation of economic growth. However, while the brand may not specifically attract visitors, intensive marketing campaigns post-listings may increase visitation, indicating that marketing the site itself to a broader audience may induce sufficient tourist activity to the site, so long as the marketing is honest and avoids hyperbole.

Branding in tourism

Since tourism, as Urry (2002) notes, is a collection of signs that is used to dictate the tourist gaze, it is unsurprising that marketing plays such a crucial role in destination management. Within this tourism marketing sphere, place and service brands would be essential signposts with which destinations can signal places of interest to tourists. Morgan and Pritchard (2014) argue that, in fact, destinations only exist due to tourist visitation and marketing narratives. Ryan and Silvanto (2014, p. 331) note that "destination brands possess unique qualities because of their association with a geographical location and unique historical and cultural setting or an exceptional natural environment." According to Keller and Lehmann (2006, p. 740), "for customers, brands can simplify choices, promise a particular quality level, reduce risk, and/or engender trust." Bigné et al. (2001, p. 613) highlighted that

> an improvement in the overall image of a place held by an individual enhances his or her intention to return and to recommend in the future. It also increases the propensity to make a positive assessment of the stay and to perceive a higher quality.

However, this assessment can be negatively impacted by a mismatch between the advertised destination and the reality upon visitation, and, thus, it is necessary for a brand to be realistic in its presentation (Govers & Go, 2009, p. 175). Therefore, an honest, positive brand image can promote repeat visitation and enhance a visitor's positive view of the visit.

Brands, however, perform complex functions for consumers, as can be seen in de Chernatony and McWilliam (1989, pp. 164–165), who identified two aspects of brand character: "representationality" and "functionality." Representationality "describes consumers' needs for brands to help express something about themselves," while functionality focuses on the brand's "functional capabilities and physical attributes" (de Chernatony & McWilliam, 1989, pp. 164–165). The representational aspects are elaborated in Aaker (1999), who highlights that these are multi-dimensional in nature, emphasizing the importance of the representationality aspect of a brand. To elaborate, "sometimes consumers express who they wish to be (desired self), strive to be (ideal self), or believe they should be (ought self), rather than who they consistently are across situations" (Aaker, 1999, p. 47). Representationality and functionality are the two brand qualities that comprise the brand box model, which illustrates the impact level, ranging from high to low, of these two aspects (de Chernatony & McWilliam, 1989). Clarke (2000) applied this model to tourism-specific service brands, which all fell within the high-functionality/high-representationality segment. This indicates that tourism-specific service brands represent not only a consumer's ideal lifestyle but also a high level of product quality. However, when applied to destination branding at country , region , and city levels, the results are quite different. Caldwell and Freire (2004, p. 59) found that "countries are so functionally diverse that they are perceived in terms of representational parts of their brand identity, while regions and cities, being smaller in scale, are perceived more from a functional point of view."

Therefore, while regions and cities are consumed based on their services and amenities, countries are visited in order to articulate some aspect of the tourist's self. In addition to functional and representational needs, Hakala et al. (2011) found that brands were required to be relatable on a cultural level as well. The interplay between a brand and cultural heritage is of particular importance in an international tourism market, wherein destinations generally try to market themselves to a broad spectrum of visitors with varying backgrounds. Similar trends have been observed in previous tourism studies. Poria et al. (2006, p. 324) indicated that visitors who felt personally connected to a site's heritage were more interested "in learning, feeling emotional involvement, being connected to their heritage and passing the legacy on to their children." Therefore, it is unsurprising that cultural distance would also play a role in destination branding. According to Ng et al. (2007, p. 1499), it is important to highlight how a destination is culturally similar to a potential visitor in order to maximize marketing impact, especially as "there is evidence that tourists may experience culture shock when visiting culturally distant destinations." Cultural proximity can also play a role, even if the temporal aspect is far removed from the visitor's contemporary reality. McIntosh and Prentice (1999, p. 608) found that domestic visitors to industrial revolution-themed "historical theme parks" benefited on a personal level due to "the reaffirmation of identity through an understanding of a person's place in time and space."

This implies that the more familiar or personally relatable a destination is, the more attractive it will be. In the USA, Kim et al. (2007) observed that cultural tourism consumption practices are still driven by visitors' "habitus." Therefore, tourists are motivated to participate in the same cultural activities that they normally engage in while at home. Furthermore, they indicated that "a certain level of cultural capital (cultural/aesthetic knowledge or taste)" was essential in order to appreciate certain types of cultural activities, such as museums, opera, and art galleries (Kim et al., 2007, p. 1370). Kerstetter et al. (2001) referred to these individual tourists as "specialists" who accumulated more site-specific knowledge prior to visiting. Due to this increased intellectual familiarity, these "specialists" were more likely to be pleased with their visitor experience (Kerstetter et al., 2001). This is echoed in McKercher (2002), whose tourist typologies were discussed in the previous chapter. McKercher (2002) found that destinations with a strong tourism brand presence will be more likely to attract purposeful and sightseeing tourists in comparison to those without a real destination brand.

This does not imply, though, that sites which are far outside the comfort and cultural spheres of tourists will not be able to attract visitors.

Leiper (1990) suggests that, within tourism systems, there exist destination "nuclei" that vary in strength of visitor attraction. The most important, or primary nuclei, would have the strongest pull factors, as was noted by Lew and McKercher (2006, p. 411) who stated that "tourists feel obliged to visit primary attractions, even if they are located in relatively out of the way places." However, primary and all subsequent levels of nuclei can only be recognized through the use of a "generating marker" in order to stimulate a desire to visit within a potential tourist (Leiper, 1990, p. 379). Nevertheless, it needs to be emphasized that "within a nuclear mix, different nuclei are likely to have different degrees of significance, because some attractions are more important than others for an individual tourist or for a group" (Leiper, 1990, p. 374). Thus while tourists may be attracted to the same nucleus, they will have different expectations regarding their visit. Furthermore, even if there are high levels of awareness, they may not necessarily lead to visitation as "awareness results, at best, in curiosity that can lead to interest and eventually to trial" (Milman & Pizam, 1995, p. 27). Additionally, lower levels of awareness can lead to an even greater lack of interest wherein nonimportant sites "are typified by convenience-based, low involvement decisions, or happenstance encounters" (Lew & McKercher, 2006, p. 411). Therefore, strong tourism brands can assist in the development of primary tourist sites, which can function as an attractor, even when the tourist lacks personal ties to the location.

The World Heritage brand

As tourism brands can be understood as signposts guiding potential visitors to primary and peripheral zones of potential interest, World Heritage sites should be easily recognizable as primary nuclei, given their purported inherent "universal" value. This is often stressed by UNESCO itself as, following inscription on the World Heritage List, States Parties are expected to ensure that the site is sufficiently marked as an official World Heritage site, though "at the country's cost and with no assurance that visitors will recognize its meaning" (Di Giovine, 2009, p. 215). Thus, UNESCO also promotes the concept of World Heritage as a branding exercise, irrespective of its actual recognition. According to Rakic and Chambers (2007, p. 146), "World Heritage Site status has become a measure of quality assurance, a trademark and an 'authenticity stamp' for the heritage tourist and an arena for the presentation of prestigious national heritage." For King and Halpenny (2014, p. 1), the World Heritage brand "signals to the public a property so irreplaceable to humankind that its values must be sustained intact in perpetuity for the benefit of future generations." Thus it would appear that the World Heritage brand functions at a level above and beyond other national, or perhaps even international, destination brands. In fact, Ryan and Silvanto (2011, p. 306) go even further by calling it an actual "seal of approval," which, as the status is bestowed by an international organization with global recognition, could potentially result in significant benefits for those countries that invest in this type recognition.

This, in part, can explain the interest from less developed countries "who often have lower levels of global visibility . . . [and] use the [World Heritage List] as a way of making their countries visible" (Timothy & Nyaupane, 2009, p. 11). Inscription is assumed to bring international prestige, as World Heritage has become "an important yardstick for adjudging the reputation of States," especially in more developed countries that do not require financial support for their listed sites' protection (Zacharias, 2008, p. 1840). This has been observed in Malaysia, where Lai and Ooi (2015) noted that city branding has become focused on the acquisition and use of the World Heritage brand. This is symptomatic of what Ashworth and van der Aa (2006, p. 154) identified as a current trend, wherein "world heritage designation is often treated by national planning agencies as if it were an extra category or class of heritage to be added to those that already exist at national or local level." The perceived importance of the brand was visible in the New South Wales government submission to the House of Representatives Standing Committee on Environment, Recreation, and the Arts inquiry into World Heritage, wherein the second point made emphasizes "the international prestige these listed properties enjoy as tourist destinations . . . Consequently a 'listing' . . . can increase marketability and comparative advantage of an area as a tourist destination" (Strategic Planning Division, 1995, p. 1). Therefore, regardless of the fact that World Heritage listing was not originally intended as a branding exercise, List membership has become synonymous with the development of a recognizable tourist marker.

This emphasis on World Heritage as a unique destination brand was highlighted by Frey and Steiner (2010, p. 9) who stated that "a site not on the UNESCO List is, by definition, not quite first, but rather second rate . . . The tourist industry understands well that not being on the List is a considerable disadvantage." For heritage tourism, the brand is assumed to function as an internationally recognizable representation of an "authentic" heritage experience that "testifies to historic attributes and developments that tourists, in many cases, would be unable to discern for themselves" (Ryan & Silvanto, 2011, p. 309). According to Musitelli (2002, p. 331), "World Heritage sites represent 15 to 20 percent of tourist destinations." However, it is unclear as to whether or not this is due to the inclusion of a site on the List or if the listing itself is a result of these sites' already high levels of visitation. Lee (2010, p. 9) noted, "While it is difficult to ascertain that tourism is a direct consequence of a World Heritage award, the fact remains that heritage sites are increasingly being commercialised through tourism development." Unsurprisingly, van der Aa (2005, p. 133) found that countries in which there is a higher level of dependency on tourism in general have a higher level of investment in getting their sites listed, as "world heritage status is a big business." These countries, including those who are "already much-represented" on the World Heritage List, are continuously putting forth new sites for inclusion on the list in comparison with less tourism-centric countries (van der Aa, 2005, p. 133).

The World Heritage brand, then, is built on the premise of universality, global importance, and unique experience. However, these qualities can also cause problems, in particular, with brand transmission. Hall and Piggin (2003) emphasize that there is not a universal understanding of the World Heritage List or heritage itself at the level of the individual tourist. The Global Strategy has attempted, in part, to remedy some of this disconnect between different cultural perceptions of "heritage," but there is still a significant amount of work that needs to be done on this topic. This is symptomatic of the complexity of the World Heritage brand, which is only further complicated through its actual application. For example, depending on the size of the site, the brand can function as either a destination or attraction marker. This, combined with the requirement that the sites be singular in nature, further muddles the potential positioning of the World Heritage brand within de Chernatony and McWilliam's (1989) brand box model. Given the importance of universality but an emphasis also on uniqueness, functionality may not be the appropriate lens through which to view its use by tourists, regardless of the scale at which it is functioning, with the brand working at a purely representational level. This can be seen in Chapter 2, wherein there was an identified potential subset of visitors who may collect World Heritage sites (Buckley, 2002, 2004; King & Prideaux, 2010; Timothy, 1998). However, as shown by King and Prideaux (2010), "collecting" World Heritage sites is not a widespread phenomenon among tourists. Therefore, it is necessary to fully understand the overall impact of the World Heritage brand among all visitors, not just the specialized collectors, as the brand can only be considered legitimate when it is actually recognized by the consumer, or in this case the tourist.

There are multiple studies that have done precisely this, but, interestingly, there has been no obvious consensus as to whether or not the brand functions at all. As may be expected, there are many studies which provide a positive assessment of the World Heritage brand. While most of these have focused more specifically on site- or national-level data, Su and Lin (2014) took a more global approach by analyzing international tourist arrivals in relation to the number of World Heritage sites within a sample of 66 nations. Their data indicated that the relationship between World Heritage and tourist arrivals formed a "U-shaped pattern" (Su & Lin, 2014, p. 57). This indicates that countries with either no or very few World Heritage sites will see noticeable increases in their international tourist arrivals, but, for those nations that already have a reasonably large number of World Heritage sites, the growth of international tourist arrivals is significantly less conspicuous, if not almost completely nonexistent. Their research indicated that 21 was the magic number of World Heritage sites needed in order to be able to regain obvious growth in international tourist arrivals. Essentially, "this increase means that when a country possesses sufficient [World Heritage sites], the 'gearing effect' of [World Heritage sites] will emerge" (Su & Lin, 2014, p. 57). This would appear to support the conceptualization of the World Heritage List as a tourism brand, albeit with its success dependent on the preexisting listings within a given country.

Visitation data has also been used within national contexts in order to support the success of the World Heritage brand in relation to tourism growth. In Italy, Patuelli et al. (2013) observed that a new World Heritage inscription could increase domestic visitation to a region by 4%, which stresses the use of the World Heritage brand as a means by which regions can differentiate themselves. In China, Yang et al. (2010, p. 834) found that the addition of one new World Heritage inscription would attract approximately six times more international tourists than a site newly branded with a high-quality national tourist marker. In both of these studies, the focus has been on broader visitor trend data, but many other studies have instead focused specifically on site-level analyses in order to assess how the brand works "on the ground." For example, Hall and Piggin (2002) specifically sought to assess local business perceptions of the World Heritage brand's impact at two sites in New Zealand: Tongariro National Park and Southwest New Zealand. While their research found no definitive, hard data-driven proof that World Heritage inscription had an impact on local businesses, "World Heritage was believed by the businesses to have had a positive or extremely positive effect on three-quarters of businesses" (Hall & Piggin, 2002, p. 410). Interestingly, although only half of business owners thought that the listing had had a positive impact on tourism in the area, 80% felt that the World Heritage brand would work as a tourist attractor.

When attempting to assess the impact of the World Heritage brand, a demand-driven method may be more appropriate, particularly as tourist visitation numbers can be impacted by external factors independent of the site's World Heritage status. Previous studies that have undertaken site-level research have tended to focus on two specific aspects of World Heritage branding: awareness and its impact on pre-trip decision making. An Australian example of awareness studies can be seen in Moscardo et al.

(2001), wherein 90% of their visitor sample exhibited awareness of the Great Barrier Reef's World Heritage status, albeit without any differentiation between different visitor's origins – i.e., domestic or international. Differentiation between local, domestic, and international visitors, however, can sometimes lead to interesting results. For example, in China, Su and Wall's (2016) research on the Temple of Heaven illustrated that most locals and three-quarters of domestic visitors were aware of the site's World Heritage status, which is in stark contrast to the less than half of international tourists who knew the site was on the List. In some instances, World Heritage awareness can be moderate but have a strong impact on those who are aware, as was seen in Palau-Saumell et al. (2012). They noted that only approximately half of visitors to La Sagrada Família in Spain were aware of the site's World Heritage status, but for those with higher levels of awareness, "any action on the heritage building or improvement of its contents will have a much greater effect on emotions and will result in greater satisfaction among the tourists that know the heritage site is a UNESCO [World Heritage site]" (Palau-Saumell et al., 2012, p. 373). In other words, there was a noted connection between World Heritage–aware visitors and the physical World Heritage site.

World Heritage brand awareness levels, however, are not always a good indicator as to whether or not the brand actually attracted visitors. This is not to say that this has never been observed. In their study of international visitors to Huangshan, China, Yan and Morrison (2008) highlighted that, while most of the foreign tourists were unaware of the site's World Heritage status, 67.1% of those who were specified that the World Heritage brand had at least partially impacted on their decision to visit the area. However, their findings appear to be the exception, as can be seen in numerous other studies. In Laos, while a high number of visitors to Luang Prabang were aware that the site was on the World Heritage List, over half stated that it was not a deciding factor (Lenaertes, 2016). In comparison, at Sagarmatha National Park in Nepal, the awareness levels were much lower, with slightly more than half of all respondents having known the site's status prior to visiting, and approximately two-thirds of visitors noting that this World Heritage status had no impact on their decision to visit (Baral et al., 2017). Even lower levels of impact were observed in Quebec City, Canada. Marcotte and Bourdeau (2006) found that, while approximately 55% of their interviewed visitors were aware of the city's World Heritage status, only 15% indicated that this influenced their decision to visit. These studies highlight that while awareness may be higher, this is no indication as to the actual effectiveness of the brand in relation to tourism growth.

However, the assumption that the World Heritage brand is a tourist magnet is widespread in the literature, and this has, on occasion, led even the academics who research the topic to question their own data. This is visible in Cuccia et al. (2016) who, using hotel nights as their data source, noted that the presence of World Heritage sites within a specific area had a negative impact on tourism destinations. For Cuccia et al. (2016), the problems associated with listing in Italy are related in part to incorrect assumptions regarding the effectiveness of the World Heritage brand, which can cause a destination to become overdeveloped, providing tourist services for a much larger visitor population than is actually received. This is then compounded by the local political environment, where the sole focus is on the attainment of "international recognition" to the detriment of proper public-private planning for sustainable tourism (Cuccia et al., 2016, p. 506). However, while this may be true to some extent, the lack of criticality toward the brand power of World Heritage is particularly problematic, especially as there are several studies that do indicate that World Heritage can have a negative impact on Italian destinations (Lo Piccolo et al., 2012; Ribaudo & Figini, 2017), and, in general, there is still no incontrovertible proof that World Heritage inscription directly increases visitation (Hall & Piggin, 2003).

The confusion surrounding the World Heritage brand is best illustrated in a study undertaken by Poria et al. (2013), which surveyed visitors in Israel. They found that respondents were unable to identify the World Heritage logo while concurrently extoling the virtue of the World Heritage List as a "global recommendation to visit" (Poria et al., 2013, p. 273). Given the previously discussed findings, it becomes clear as to why Cellini (2011) would have chosen to question and ultimately reanalyze Yang et al.'s (2010) data. This led to his dismissal of their findings by taking the oppositional position that "UNESCO recognition appears to be ineffective in fostering international tourist arrivals" (Cellini, 2011, p. 453). Furthermore, even in instances where there are observable impacts, they are not evenly distributed across different sites, with some sites still receiving minimal visitation (Buckley, 2004; Hall & Piggin, 2001; Tisdell & Wilson, 2002). Thus it becomes clear that understanding the impact, if any, of the World Heritage brand is exceedingly complex.

Part of the problem with studies that observe significant increases could be their reliance on visitation data taken immediately following a site being inscribed. This is visible in Huang et al.'s (2012, p. 46) research on Macao, wherein they discovered that World Heritage listing, and subsequent use of its marketing power, can increase tourism in the short term but has little lasting impact. This may explain why authors observe an increase in visitation when analyzing tourist numbers, but others find little impact when actually surveying visitors. Furthermore, impacts in tourism visitation may not necessarily even be a response to World Heritage listing. In fact,

Buckley (2004, p. 82), in his research on Australian World Heritage sites, noted that, based on the extant data for each site under study, "any significant increases in the growth of visitor numbers at [World Heritage Areas] seems to have coincided with periods of major environmental controversy rather than the date of [World Heritage] listing." Thus, not only is there an unfounded belief that the World Heritage List will strongly increase tourist numbers, but this, in turn, can pose economic problems when areas are overdeveloped.

The lack of long-term influence of World Heritage listing was visible in the Greater Blue Mountains World Heritage Area where, based on the findings of Hardiman and Burgin (2013), the site's status did not appear to function as a tourist attractor five years after being placed on the World Heritage List. In fact, the majority of the surveyed visitors were unaware that they had visited a World Heritage site at all. Low levels of awareness were common across all 15 studied Australian World Heritage sites, with approximately half of all respondents unable to name a single listed site (Hardiman & Burgin, 2013). Tisdell and Wilson's (2002) findings illustrate similar low World Heritage brand awareness within the Australian context and subsequent weakness of the World Heritage brand as a tourist attractor. A lack of awareness was also observed in Macao by Dewar et al. (2012, p. 325) who found that "it is clear that the average visitor has only a vague understanding of [World Heritage] and it was not a major motivator for their visit." In Japan, Jones et al. (2017, p. 75) noted that World Heritage listing appeared to have "little direct impact" on domestic hikers at Mount Fuji. The general ignorance regarding World Heritage was further emphasized in King and Halpenny's (2014) research, wherein the tourists' low levels of awareness extended to the World Heritage symbol, which many were unable to identify. Similar results were found in Poria et al.'s (2011) research on an archaeological World Heritage site in Israel. However, not only were their respondents less cognizant of the World Heritage logo, but they also appeared to be more motivated to visit sites which were not on the World Heritage List than those listed.

In certain contexts, this unawareness toward a site's World Heritage status may be more symptomatic of general perceptions of UNESCO and World Heritage. This is the case in the USA where Hazen (2008) noted that, while there was some amount of suspicion toward the international power held by UNESCO, more than 40% of her sample had no opinion on the World Heritage Convention, as they knew little about World Heritage in general. This is particularly interesting as the USA played an important role in the establishment of the World Heritage Convention and, according to Williams (2004), there are clear advantages to be gained from inscription. However, this means little to the average visitor at a US World Heritage site who is heedless of the site's World Heritage status (Williams, 2004). Smith (2002) observed a similar situation in Maritime Greenwich in relation to a lack of overall awareness of the site's World Heritage status. However, in the UK context, World Heritage inscription "appears to be valued more as a catalyst for investment, regeneration and tourism development than as a significant icon in its own right" (Smith, 2002, p. 146). Therefore, at least in the case of Greenwich, there is a modicum of acknowledgment of the potential difficulties in relying on the World Heritage List as a tourist attractor in and of itself.

Recently, Adie et al. (2018) undertook an international, cross-contextual study in order to assess the impact, if any, of the World Heritage brand across different levels of HDI. Their study, which included sites in the USA, Serbia, and Morocco, exhibited findings in line with previous research. They identified a specific group of individual tourists who had higher levels of World Heritage awareness, but they found that "[World Heritage] designation was not a strong attractor at any of the sites, indicating that there was no alteration based on the development level of the nation or the geographical location of the site" (Adie et al., 2018, p. 411). While these results mirror those found in the previously discussed studies, Adie et al. (2018) took this one step further by referring to World Heritage as a placebo brand. As was seen in their results, World Heritage awareness did not impact motivation to visit, but, regardless of the data, individuals on the supply-side of World Heritage tourism still assert that the brand brings in visitors (Ashworth & van der Aa,2006; Hall & Piggin, 2002; Leask, 2006). Thus, much like medical placebos, the World Heritage brand is seen to attract tourists merely because those on the supply-side believe it does, regardless of evidentiary proof to the contrary.

The placebo effect may be also be attributable to the findings which tend to support the impact of the World Heritage brand, which is also one of the more problematic aspects of World Heritage branding studies. Namely, unlike traditional demand-focused marketing literature, World Heritage research tends to fixate on broad trends and metadata when attempting to compare across contexts or between multiple sites. Even with a more national-level focus, such as that seen in Halpenny et al. (2015), there is a reliance on supply-side-provided data. In their research, Halpenny et al. (2015) sought to test the effectiveness of the World Heritage brand at Canadian sites through the use of localized, site-specific data, specifically visitor numbers and park fees, which were then presented along with reported communication with site managers and media coverage. They attributed the lack of impact on visitation to Canadian sites to a dearth of general awareness, which could be remedied through better marketing and education surrounding the importance of the World Heritage designation (Halpenny et al., 2015). A recent example is found in Yang et al. (2019), which sought to disprove the conclusion of Adie et al.'s (2018) visitor-driven data through an analysis of the findings from previous meta-analyses, thus continuing the over-reliance on impersonal big data dealing with visitor trends as opposed to demand-driven research "on the ground." How can the World Heritage tourist market be understood if tourists aren't asked directly what they want, know, or need?

Given the growing body of literature suggesting that the World Heritage brand's influence may have been greatly overstated, it is important to tread carefully when discussing potential post-listing tourism boons. This assumption about the strength of the World Heritage brand as a tourist magnet has been referred to as "naïve" by Fyall and Rakic (2006, p. 165), as it "overly simplifies the nature of visitor trends at World Heritage Sites." For example, according to Jones et al. (2017), the World Heritage brand may function better in the context of natural sites, as there are significantly fewer of them in contrast to cultural heritage sites, which dominate the list. This highlights another issue currently facing the list: overpopulation with a growth in sites that are no longer representative of Outstanding Universal Value (Logan, 2012). This situation may be highly problematic, particularly for those nations that are actively using or seeking to use their World Heritage sites as markers of distinction within the international tourism marketplace. Furthermore, Fyall and Rakic (2006, p. 171) noted that "overexposure of the World Heritage 'brand' is likely to dilute the benefits to be derived from such a quality 'trademark' with the source of differentiation achieved through brand recognition no longer carrying influence in the market." Thus, the constant push to inscribe more and more sites on the list, due in part to the placebo effect of the brand, is only weakening what little power the World Heritage brand actually holds. This, then, could potentially cause "tangible disadvantages at site level or places relying heavily on the tourist dollar for management and conservation revenue" (Dewar et al., 2012, p. 324).

Willingness to pay is an excellent example of the problematic nature of relying heavily on the World Heritage brand. In Nepal, Baral, Kaul et al. (2017) found that international visitors to Sagarmatha National Park, home of Mt. Everest, exhibited a statistically significant difference in relation to what they were willing to pay to enter the park, wherein tourists who knew the site was on the World Heritage List prior to arriving were willing to pay approximately 20% more than those who were unaware of the status. However, the level of awareness in general was still not high, with only a little over half knowing about the park's World Heritage status prior to visiting (Baral, Kaul et al., 2017). This indicates that, while the parks entry fees can be raised, the World Heritage–aware visitors do not constitute a large enough proportion of the visitor population to allow for their preference for higher entry fees to be implemented. However, it does signal that there is a higher value attached to the site in relation to its World Heritage status. In contrast, similar levels of awareness were seen at four natural World Heritage sites in the USA, but Hazen (2009) noted no significant relationship between willingness to pay more for entry and whether visitors knew that the site was on the World Heritage List.

In Germany, World Heritage status only resulted in a €5 (14%) increase in a visitor's willingness to pay to visit Jasmund National Park, part of the transboundary Ancient and Primeval Beech Forests of the Carpathians and Other Regions of Europe World Heritage site (Wuepper, 2017). Furthermore, based on the results of two of Wuepper's (2017) models, this increase only occurs when the World Heritage site and non-listed site are visited together. The World Heritage site by itself actually elicits a lower willingness to pay when compared to the non-listed chalk cliffs. When investigating the effectiveness of the World Heritage brand for archaeological sites in Israel, Poria et al. (2011) found that their respondents would be willing to pay more to enter a World Heritage site in comparison with a non-listed one. However, as previously discussed, these same tourists were also more likely to visit a non-listed site and were less aware of the World Heritage logo. The importance of entry fees cannot be overstated, as they are often used for conservation activities. According to Cochrane and Tapper (2006, p. 108),

> it is entirely reasonable to apply the "user pays" principle by ensuring that the tourists who benefit from visits to the sites should pay for their upkeep. At the same time, there are many reasons why site managers cannot become over-reliant on this source of income.

Those responsible for these charges, though, must be careful, as site entrance fee implementation or rate increases can be seen as a double-edged sword, with "extravagant entrance fees" being seen as a hindrance to visitation and assisting in the assignation of "negative attributes" by possible future visitors (Poria et al., 2011, p. 204).

Apart from the inability to potentially raise entry fees based purely on value perceptions of tourists, there are additional issues related to the inflation of the influence of the World Heritage brand, particularly in regard to actual visitor numbers. For example, Lo Piccolo et al. (2012, p. 271), in their research on the Aeolian Islands, found that "the strong decrease in the average stay (ratio between the number of nights spent to the number of customers) has declined from 4.52 (2000) to 3.9 (2009)." In this instance, not only did visitation not increase, but it actually declined by

13.3% nine years post-listing. Ribaudo and Figini (2017) also undertook an analysis of visitation impacts of World Heritage in Italy using municipal data from 16 sites. Based on their findings, "there is no statistical evidence whatsoever that market growth rates will accelerate, at least for the majority of destinations in a mature tourism country like Italy" (Ribaudo & Figini, 2017, p. 540). However, this lack of growth is also visible outside of Italy. In South Africa, Rogerson and van der Merwe (2016) found that, for over three-quarters of accommodation providers around the Cradle of Mankind World Heritage site, visitation specifically driven by the World Heritage site was negligible. This would appear to contradict Jansen-Verbeke and McKercher (2010, p. 192), who suggested that World Heritage would only cause "already popular places [to] become more popular." However, even if visitation does potentially increase at a specific site, "the amount of time spent at a [World Heritage site] is often as short as a few hours" (Boyd & Timothy, 2006, p. 57). As can be seen, visitation is highly variable and only further reinforces the risks associated with the continued misplaced faith in the World Heritage brand.

World Heritage marketing

Regardless of the World Heritage brand's influence, often sites are heavily marketed following their inscription. In fact, the assumption that the World Heritage brand functions as a tourist attractor, particularly when using visitation numbers as a measure of impact, completely ignores the influence of destination marketing. Countries that strive to get their sites on the World Heritage List specifically to increase tourist visitation often put a significant amount of money into the post-listing marketing of these sites. Visitation, then, would more likely be tied to the mere fact that perhaps a once unknown site is now at the forefront of foreign and domestic marketing campaigns. This interaction is visible, though not highlighted, in Jimura (2016), where the Kii World Heritage site in Japan, a heretofore unknown tourism destination, has seen an increase in visitation since listing. However, visitors to the site are unaware of the World Heritage status. Jimura (2016) also emphasized the success of the destination marketing campaign, which has been directed at foreign tourists. Therefore, there has been a growth in World Heritage–oblivious foreign visitors to a site that has been marketed more post-listing. Jimura (2016) attributed this growth to the strength of the World Heritage brand, but it is clear that the marketing strategy is the successful factor in this visitation equation.

The importance of marketing toward visitation is further illustrated by research on tourism in the Greater Blue Mountains World Heritage Area in Australia, where Lloyd et al. (2015) undertook an analysis of tourism brochures available at visitor centers found in regions that contained portions of the site. These were assessed in order to determine the extent to which World Heritage branding was incorporated into visitor information. Based on their findings, the World Heritage brand is not utilized often within the visitor brochures, both in terms of the name "World Heritage" and the logo, and that the previous brand "'Blue Mountains' was used five times more in promotional materials than 'Greater Blue Mountains'" (Lloyd et al., 2015, pp. 332–333). While it is unlikely that the use of the World Heritage brand would increase visitation to the Greater Blue Mountains, the lack of brand utilization may account for the low levels of World Heritage awareness in Hardiman and Burgin's (2013) sample. In certain instances, however, the use of the World Heritage logo and name may in fact cause more harm than good, as it focuses attention wholly on the World Heritage site to the detriment of surrounding, related heritage sites (Boyd and Timothy, 2006). Successful marketing at a World Heritage site, then, would be required to utilize the existing destination brand. This is visible in the marketing strategy of the English Lake District, which is discussed in Box 3.1.

Box 3.1   World Heritage marketing done right: the English Lake District, UK

Given the importance of marketing to tourism visitation, it is useful to see a successful branding activity that is not driven by tourism growth, and the English Lake District World Heritage Site is an excellent example. The Lake District is located in the northwest of England in Cumbria. The site spans approximately 853 square miles with a population of 41,000 in 23,000 homes (Lake District National Park Partnership, 2019a). Originally designated as a national park in 1951, the effort to place the Lake District on the World Heritage List began in 1986, although early attempts were unsuccessful, due in part to the lack of recognition of cultural landscapes in the early years of the convention. According to the official Lake District World Heritage website (Lake District National Park Partnership, 2019a), the addition of a cultural landscape as a type of World Heritage in 1993 was a reaction to the Lake District nominations. However, the site was only placed on the World Heritage List in 2017 under three criteria, II, V, and VI, for its natural beauty, continuation of traditional land use, and historical importance to the foundation of several landscape-driven movements. The current management system on-site is driven by a local approach to sustainable tourism, which is focused on local businesses and communities. In fact, they specifically state, "World Heritage Status is not about increasing visitor numbers; the Partnership wants to encourage visitors to stay longer and spend more" (Lake District National Park Partnership, 2019a). This is clearly visible in their marketing strategy. Unlike many sites that rely on the World Heritage brand as a stand-alone attractor, the Lake District has taken a very different approach. They have integrated the World Heritage label into their own site-specific marketing materials, effectively creating a separate "English Lake District World Heritage Site" brand. Furthermore, and in line with their sustainable community focus, different branding materials are available open access via an online branding toolkit (Lake District National Park Partnership, 2019b). This toolkit includes multiple logos with relevant taglines suitable for all local industries within the World Heritage site, with, a stress on the local providence of the products and services on offer. It also provides, again, open source, approved photographs, seasonal color palettes, an e-mail signature, and location-specific logos. At its launch, it already had strong support from several local business owners who stressed its usefulness for tapping into diverse markets and to illustrate the pride that local businesses have in their local area (Lake District National Park Authority, 2018). Some business owners indicated that they had already experienced some success with newly branded products, indicating that there was real visitor interest in World Heritage site items. The use of World Heritage status to create a distinctive brand that stresses the local qualities of the place may, given time, prove to be a much more successful marketing campaign, particularly for local businesses, than traditional large-scale World Heritage brand-specific ones.

Nevertheless, marketing impacts can potentially be more substantial when tourist sites are more remote, as was observed by Heldt Cassel and Pashkevich (2014). They found that when marketing World Heritage sites in Sweden, destination marketing consistently used "superlatives" to emphasize the uniqueness of the sites (Heldt Cassel & Pashkevich, 2014, p. 1631). While many sites seek to differentiate themselves from others in terms of their unique offer, Heldt Cassel and Pashkevich (2014, p. 1631) proposed that this was in part caused by the remoteness of the Swedish World Heritage site in comparison with other European sites requiring potential visitors "to be highly motivated and experienced in consuming these types of attractions." However, overly exaggerated marketing can sometimes cause problems, as was seen at the Singapore Botanic Gardens. According to Lee et al. (2018, p. 349), visitor satisfaction fell after the site was inscribed, and they hypothesized that this may have been due to the marketing strategy for the site, which "created overinflated expectations about what the Gardens offered." The use of exaggeration is visible in other World Heritage marketing, which can cause a mismatch between a visitor's expectations and reality upon visiting. The marketing of Hoi An in Vietnam is an excellent example of this. The imagery used portrays the World Heritage portion of Hoi An as an idyllic version of the past, emphasizing clean empty streets and a sense of frozen history, which contrasts with the vibrant and very much lived-in urban heritage environment (Parnwell, 2016).

Conclusion

This chapter has taken a critical approach to the use of the World Heritage brand as a tourist attractor, particularly given the reliance by some sites on the potential increases in tourist numbers. While, as has been noted, several studies have indicated that there are positive increases post-listing, these tend to be broad analyses of visitor trends that do not take into consideration either external impacts on visitation or the increased marketing activity that generally occurs following the inscription of a site. In fact, it is suggested that this intensification in regard to marketing may be the actual reason why visitor numbers grow and not, in fact, the World Heritage brand specifically. After all, according to Yang and Lin (2014, p. 84), World Heritage inscription only alters the "label" attached to a site, and, "thus, the impact of that labelling on tourism demand depends heavily on the means by which and the degree to which it is marketing by the destination authority." This would explain why countries such as the USA, which doesn't overtly market post-listing, or Italy, which tends to have a laissez-faire marketing approach, may not see alterations in visitation numbers.

4   Holistic World Heritage management

Introduction

While the past chapters have mainly concentrated on the demand-side of World Heritage tourism, this chapter will delve into the supply-side, specifically focusing on the management of World Heritage sites. As has been mentioned in the introductory chapter of this book, management is one of the requirements for inscription as a World Heritage site and is intrinsically tied to the other three additional criteria – namely, site integrity, protection, and, in the case of cultural sites, authenticity. The need for adequate management has been stressed from the inception of the list, but it truly came to the forefront in 2005 with the introduction of an explicit requirement for management plans at all World Heritage sites. This meant that all future sites would need to present a management plan for approval prior to being considered for inclusion. The organization of this chapter has been developed following a thorough review of the literature through which three specific themes emerged – namely, planning and policy (Planning), site-specific and place-based dynamics (Place), and local community and tourist-related considerations (People). These issues are all interrelated but have distinct requirements when discussing World Heritage management in a holistic fashion. They also reflect UNESCO's movement toward the inclusion of sustainable development within the World Heritage system, as is notable from their creation of a sustainable development policy document (UNESCO, 2015). The interconnectedness of these factors is visible in Figure 4.1, which also stresses the equal importance of each aspect.

Planning

The World Heritage governance system

Planning and good governance are essential to the implementation of a successful management system at World Heritage sites. Therefore, prior

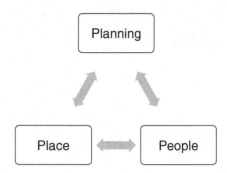

Figure 4.1 Holistic World Heritage management

to a discussion of the management structure and practices used at site or regional levels, it is necessary to outline the World Heritage governance system, which was the direct result of the signing of the World Heritage Convention in 1972 and led to the development of an international heritage governance model. While the World Heritage Convention was established in order to protect and conserve natural and cultural sites deemed of Outstanding Universal Value, it also set in place a legal framework that created a system of heritage norms to which States Parties that have signed the convention should conform (Francioni & Lenzerini, 2008). However, these norms can be difficult to enforce, as the concept of state sovereignty is strongly present throughout the convention (Francioni & Lenzerini, 2008). This can appear contradictory as the convention itself promotes the idea of heritage, which is internationally significant, while simultaneously placing the onus for its management and protection entirely under the control of the national government in which it is situated (Francioni, 2008). This results in a fairly complex, multi-scalar governance system, but, before commencing with a discussion of this system, it should be noted that, for the purposes of this chapter, governance is "the management of the common affairs of political communities" as defined by Healey (2006, p. 59).

As has been noted, the World Heritage governance system is multi-scalar, and, at the macro-level, the governance structure is notably different from the broader system. There has been a marked shift away from heritage conservation, which, as has been noted, is the ultimate purpose of the World Heritage Convention (Logan, 2012; Meskell, 2013, 2015; Meskell et al., 2015). Several authors (James & Winter, 2017; Logan, 2012; Meskell, 2013, 2015; Meskell et al., 2015, Schmitt, 2009) have also highlighted a growth in the use of informal networking as a means to secure specific results during committee meetings. These activities, combined with an increasing emphasis on political influence, are representative of Healey's (2006) clientelism. According to Healey (2006, p. 229), "elected politicians and officials become critical gatekeepers in managing the direction of the flow of resources." This type of governance can often result in backroom dealing, which was visible in the listing process of the Bolgar Historical and Archaeological Complex in Russia. According to Plets (2015), Bolgar was listed against the express recommendation of ICOMOS as a direct result of the support of Russian economic partners. However, this is unsurprising given the "increasing disregard for expert advice" within the World Heritage Committee (Willems, 2014, p. 116) and the shift from heritage experts to "career diplomats" at the committee level (Brumann, 2014, p. 2177). It should be noted that while this clientelism is becoming prevalent at the macro-level, the broader World Heritage governance system does not function in this manner.

Given the ways in which the convention is implemented and the World Heritage Committee interacts with the individual States Parties, the broader World Heritage governance system is best defined as a hierarchical network mode of governance (Jessop, 2011). This is, in some ways, unsurprising given the treaty's origins within a Western democratic context, wherein representative democracy is perceived as the optimal political system (Healey, 2006). Healey (2006, p. 221) defines hierarchical network governance as a "model [that] encourages the development of hierarchically-structured bureaucracies, focused around technical and administrative expertise, in which officials justify their actions and decisions upwards to their seniors and the politicians to whom these are accountable." This model is characterized by a top-down, goal-oriented policy approach (Jessop, 2011) with defined power relationships (Hall, 2011). It is comparable to the political archetype of territorial governance where the outer layers of governance (global/state) look inward to regional and destination governance levels (Bramwell & Lane, 2011; Hall, 2011; Pechlaner & Volgger, 2013).

Below the Committee level, the World Heritage Convention created the general structure of World Heritage governance, but it does not provide any definitive guidance in relation to how, specifically, the World Heritage List should be managed. This is instead provided by the Operational Guidelines, which detail the norms for the nomination, inscription, and management of sites. These norms "are a genuine example of soft law, as they are applied with preference to equivalent national rules during the process of nomination, as well as for monitoring and reporting activities" (Galera, 2016, p. 240). They are the practical implementation of the legal framework set out in the World Heritage Convention, which aligns with Healey's (2006) portrayal of management as a collective activity of governance. However, the convention's prioritization of state sovereignty can result in governance clashes, particularly when the highly varied governance modes found within the States Parties do not integrate well with the other levels within the World Heritage governance process (Hall, 2008). For example, the Tropical Rainforest Heritage of Sumatra in Indonesia has a disparate management system due to the fact that the World Heritage site is composed of three separate parks that are found across eight different provinces and a myriad of local districts (Cochrane, 2016a). Given the various issues at all levels, this results in ineffective site-wide management. Therefore, these risks need to be taken into account given the multi-scalar nature of the World Heritage system, wherein good governance is essential to ensure good management. Fortunately, very few sites are transboundary, and thus the national legal structure dictates the different roles within the World Heritage governance framework.

It is important to keep in mind that the World Heritage governance structure is not as static as it appears. Recently, there have been noted shifts away from top-down governance toward a more participatory approach through the integration of multiple stakeholders (Hughes et al., 2016; UNESCO, 2017). However, this is not to say that that style of governance no longer exists within the World Heritage system, as can be seen at the Great Wall World Heritage site in Badaling, China (Su & Wall, 2012). This is in part due to socio-political differences across nation states. China, for example, has a very different conceptualization of what local involvement entails and traditionally has functioned in a very top-down manner (Su & Wall, 2015) as can be seen in their World Heritage nominations (Chi et al., 2017, p. 210; Su et al., 2016; Sun et al., 2017). Hierarchical systems also exist in other World Heritage contexts – i.e., Indonesia (Cochrane, 2016a), Italy (Borgarino et al., 2016), and Turkey (Human, 2015). In Turkey, the top-down system has created mechanisms whereby local stakeholders have limited power within the development of World Heritage management processes (Human, 2015). Interestingly, based on the work undertaken by Conradin and Wiesmann (2015) who compared the impact of World Heritage designation on conservation measures at natural sites in the global South and North (for definitions, see p. 691), the management of the sites in the global South is heavily top-down with approximately 75% of the sites directly managed by a central government body. Thus, while the general shift within the broader World Heritage system is trending toward a more bottom-up approach, this will potentially encounter problems when there is an attempt to implement these policies within the more traditional, hierarchical States Parties.

In comparison, there are many countries that are attempting to apply the bottom-up approach, albeit to varying levels of success. In Italy, for example, the heritage governance structure is strongly centralized, but there have been calls for stronger integration of the private sector within the heritage management structure as a way in which to improve management and access to resources (Boggio, 2000). This is already being implemented in the Crespi d'Adda World Heritage site where a new management plan involving a multi-stakeholder approach is in development (Borgarino et al., 2016). However, there are still some problems with the application of this governance style in the Italian context. For example, the site of Herculaneum has already had some success through bottom-up management and public-private partnerships, but the public sector appears to be disinclined to "increase ties between the site and local community" (Thompson, 2007, p. 5). The reliance on these top-down structures could be a result of "a dependence on central governments to provide resources and the potential lack of administrative capacity of sub-levels to carry out planned activities" within multi-scalar governance systems (Elmi & Hinna, 2017, p. 242). As can be seen, while there has been a concerted effort in some systems to undertake a more participatory approach, there are still some "growing pains."

Even the successful realization of a participatory approach is not without its own problems, however, which may be due to the complexity involved in the implementation process. According to Liburd and Becken (2017, p. 1724),

> the formal governance arrangements at UNESCO World Heritage Sites are often complemented by stewardship that involves alliances across local, national and international levels. Appreciating the dynamic nature of tourism in World Heritage Areas, these alliances are constituted in and through shifting ideologies, government, global capital, position and the persons influencing policies.

The integration of all of these factors is possible, but not without some difficulty, as was observed in the case of Terschelling, located in the Dutch segment of the Wadden Sea World Heritage site. Some stakeholders at this site highlighted the problems associated with local-level decision making, which are predominantly caused by the occasional inability of the local municipality to enact changes due to both structural and resource-poor restrictions (Heslinga et al., 2017). However, the problems identified indicate that, at least, the system at the Wadden Sea is multi-stakeholder at its core. Another example of multi-stakeholder planning is visible in Rodwell's (2002) study on industrial World Heritage sites in the UK that ensured that their management plans were developed in collaboration with a myriad of stakeholders, non-governmental and local, as well as public and private.

Overall, the implementation of this approach has had mixed results, and this is due in part to a lack of acknowledgment of the contexts, both place and people based.

World Heritage management plans

While World Heritage management is notably context specific, as will be discussed in the next section focused on place, there are several overarching requirements that must be met regardless of the site's specificities. Once a nominated site has succeeded in being approved for inscription, the World Heritage Committee assigns a Statement of Outstanding Universal Value, which "shall be the basis for the future protection and management of the property" (UNESCO, 2017, p. 41). Currently, in order to safeguard each site's Outstanding Universal Value, the Operational Guidelines (2017, p. 31) require "an appropriate management plan or other documented management system" to be in place prior to listing. This requirement, though, is not without its critics. For example, Ripp and Rodwell (2017) found the use of management plans problematic due to their impersonal, hierarchical nature derived from Western business models. They instead call for the implementation of management systems that are holistic in nature with a people-centric approach, which is interesting, as this is, in fact, how management structures should be functioning as per the Operational Guidelines (UNESCO, 2017). As has already been noted, this has only been a requirement since 2005, and thus management structures "on the ground" at many World Heritage sites may differ from the ideals promoted in the Operational Guidelines or may not be well developed at all, especially in the case of older inscriptions. However, even for sites that may be less well managed, the requirements surrounding protection and preservation of the site's Outstanding Universal Value remain, placing the onus of responsibility on the appropriate state, or states in the case of transboundary World Heritage.

This obligation often comes with high financial costs both pre-and post-inscription, which could be seen as a hindrance for States Parties on the lower end of the HDI. VanBlarcom and Kayahan (2011, p. 146) identified the costs as follows:

In order to apply to be a World Heritage site, first, sites go through a bidding process, where they submit a nomination form demonstrating that they meet the [World Heritage site] criteria set by UNESCO World Heritage Centre. The bidding process entails costs associated with the preparation of the management plan, conducting supportive studies and consultation provided by third parties. Second, sites that successfully receive the [World Heritage site] inscription would incur costs in order to meet UNESCO requirements such as monitoring, periodic reporting and maintenance of the sites. Finally, there are costs associated with the [World Heritage] status-related activities that are difficult to quantify since they are site specific.

Therefore, it would be safe to assume that those sites that are located in countries, which do not already have heritage protection measures due to monetary restrictions, would potentially encounter difficulties in securing sufficient funding to support this process, even with external assistance. Thus the results of the listing would have to be highly beneficial to the States Party in order to proceed with the potentially costly World Heritage process.

As was observed by VanBlarcom and Kayahan (2011), additional costs arise during periodic reporting cycles, which, similarly to general management and protection policies, are the responsibility of the States Parties. As such, they can be viewed as an additional expense that a nation may incur after already having had to prepare the site for nomination, which for some countries can mean a complete management overhaul to conform to UNESCO's expectations. However, periodic reporting is an important process as it is used by UNESCO to assess the extent to which States Parties are fulfilling their responsibilities toward their listed sites. Additionally, from a broader preservation and management perspective, it can be very informative for UNESCO, as the main goals behind this exercise are

a) to provide an assessment of the application of the *World Heritage Convention* by the State Party;
b) to provide an assessment as to whether the Outstanding Universal Value of the properties inscribed on the World Heritage List is being maintained over time;
c) to provide up-dated information about the World Heritage properties to record the changing circumstances and state of conservation of the properties;
d) to provide a mechanism for regional co-operation and exchange of information and experiences between States Parties concerning the implementation of the *Convention* and World Heritage conservation.

(UNESCO, 2017, p. 54)

This monitoring process not only allows UNESCO to have a sense of what is happening "on the ground" but also to identify potential problems that may otherwise have been missed. This can allow UNESCO to directly intervene, where necessary, as States Parties are responsible for all of the costs of site maintenance and protection unless there is some perceived immediate threat.

If there is a threat, there are several possible responses, including training and assistance in finding external funding. However, in certain instances, UNESCO also can provide financial aid through the World Heritage Fund. According to Vrdoljak (2008, p. 221), "it is the possibility of financial and technical assistance which has proved an additional incentive for states to sign up to the convention." Unfortunately, the World Heritage Fund is chronically underfunded, consisting of only approximately four million US dollars per annum, which is a paltry sum when compared with the number of sites that are actually currently on the World Heritage List (Musitelli, 2002). It should be noted that priority is given to the following:

- A Least Developed Country or Low Income Economy as defined by the United Nations Economic and Social Council's Committee for Development Policy, or
- A Lower Middle Income Country as defined by the World Bank, or
- A Small Island Developing State (SIDS), or
- A State Party in a post-conflict situation.

(UNESCO, 2017, p. 59)

Thus there is a certain level of monetary assistance available for those States Parties that most need it as well as the assistance of associated NGOs. Notwithstanding this preferential treatment, it needs to be noted again that the actual amount available in the World Heritage Fund is not sufficient for the quantity of sites on the World Heritage List. This is in part caused by what Frey et al. (2013, p. 3) refer to as an "overextension of the List," wherein UNESCO, due to never having instituted a maximum number of sites, becomes progressively responsible for overseeing increasingly more sites, stretching their budget thinner and thinner. Therefore, "greater protection of, or additional financial resources from UNESCO to, the enlisted properties" is no longer a given (Bertacchini & Saccone, 2012, p. 330).

Due to the insufficiency of the World Heritage Fund, the States Parties have become significantly more important to the preservation of the World Heritage List. In an analysis of the legal implications of the World Heritage List, Zacharias (2008, p. 1840) emphasized that it is the international community's (i.e. the States Parties) responsibility to provide monetary and/ or other forms of support to those who are unable to adequately protect or conserve their heritage. The signatories of the World Heritage Convention, therefore, are considered more responsible than the actual organization for upholding the priorities of the convention although the extent to which it has been enacted in domestic law remains a moot point. This is not to say that listing does not provide any access to funding. Frey et al. (2013, p. 3) highlight that one of the largest benefits of being listed relates to the increased attention from potential funding sources, which in turn results in better methods of protection, and, although this monetary supply is insufficient in the face of current demand, it still may help sites that are particularly vulnerable. This is especially important, as sites that do not address conservation issues risk being placed on the List of World Heritage in Danger or even be delisted.

As has been seen, these standardized management requirements are almost entirely focused on the preservation of a site's Outstanding Universal Value, which is inherent to the protection of the World Heritage brand, as was seen in the previous chapter. This management dynamic led Adie (2017) to frame the overarching management structure of World Heritage as a franchise system, wherein the States Parties "purchase" the right to brand their sites as World Heritage. This reinforces the power dynamic emphasized throughout this discussion regarding general management regulations – namely, the importance of the States Parties in relation to actual responsibility toward listed World Heritage sites. Additionally, the franchise model compliments the previously discussed World Heritage governance system, as it allows for a variety of governance styles and stresses the sovereignty of States Parties. Furthermore, the use of a franchise system model allows for multiple local contexts and site-specific needs so long as they deliver on the qualities promised by the World Heritage brand. This is especially important given the importance of place and locality to the overall management of individual World Heritage sites.

Place

While the listing process includes criteria that are intangible, the World Heritage List is decidedly tangible in nature, with a fixed spatial component. Therefore, place should be considered an essential aspect of the management process. Place in this sense is the situated geographic location of the site as well as its socio-cultural context. Although the sites themselves are of Outstanding Universal Value, implying that their importance is, in the end, global, the reasons for listing are inherently tied to the local context, both contemporary and historical. This results in what Salazar (2014, p. 42) calls "pluriversality" or the diversity of meanings assigned to the site by a variety of individuals and groups, albeit with the micro-local level taking precedence in relation to practicalities on-site. Thus, it is unsurprising that management of sites would be highly dependent on their specific geographic locations. This is not to say that the site-specific measures put in place would contrast those from the larger governance structure and management regulations, but they do allow for a more customized approach to protection of the Outstanding Universal Value, which, as has been noted, is global in importance but local in context. These protective measures are essential, as has been discussed previously, to the continuation of the site's presence on the World Heritage List, which is tied to the need for World Heritage sites to be passed down to future generations (Buckley, 2018; Human, 2015).

In order to protect Outstanding Universal Value in whatever manner is most appropriate, a site-specific tourism management plan must be developed for each World Heritage property. These may be multi-faceted in nature in the case of serial sites or include multi-scalar management plans when the serial sites are also transboundary (i.e., the Architectural Work of Le Corbusier, an Outstanding Contribution to the Modern Movement; Ancient and Primeval Beech Forests of the Carpathians and Other Regions of Europe; Qhapaq Ñan, Andean Road System). While these plans often have transnational governance aspects, which have been discussed in the previous section, they should also include more localized, property-specific management structures. It is these localized aspects of World Heritage site management that are dictated by a place-centric focus. This is particularly apparent when discussing tourism management at the site level, as all sites will have their own specificities that need to be addressed. It should be noted that not all sites will require significant tourism management plans, particularly those which are extremely difficult, prohibitively expensive, or especially dangerous to visit (i.e., Bikini Atoll, New Zealand Subantartic Islands, Ancient City of Damascus). However, the vast majority of World Heritage sites are not only accessible but also host at least a moderate number of tourists. In acknowledgment of the relationship between tourism and World Heritage sites, UNESCO created the World Heritage and Sustainable Tourism program in 2010. This program's mission is to "facilitate the management and development of sustainable tourism at World Heritage properties through fostering increased awareness, capacity, and balanced participation of all stakeholders in order to protect the properties and their Outstanding Universal Value" (UNESCO, n.d.-b).

The Sustainable Tourism Program's development stems from the need to balance site preservation with site use, particularly as tourism is not always sufficiently planned, as was observed in Job et al.'s (2017) research on natural World Heritage site management. A lack of planning is also visible in Phong Nha-Ke Bang National Park in Vietnam. According to Lien (2016, p. 302), tourist visitation to the park is uncontrolled, resulting in a push to grow tourist numbers, which in turn is putting additional pressure on the park's already fragile ecosystem. However, threats can arise not merely from direct tourist activity but also from associated ones, such as the development of infrastructure around the site, as was seen in Phong Nha-Ke Bang National Park (Lien, 2016) and Sumatra (Cochrane, 2016a).

Therefore, the strict management of tourism and related external activities is highly important in order to ensure the preservation of the site's Outstanding Universal Value. However, even in instances where Outstanding Universal Value is under threat, alterations in the management system can assist in the alleviation of some of the risks from tourism, as can be seen in the example of Belize in Box 4.1.

Box 4.1   Successful management interventions: Belize Barrier Reef Reserve System, Belize

The Belize Barrier Reef Reserve System (BBRRS) provides an excellent example of planning and management in the face of substantial risks to a World Heritage site. The BBRRS is Belize's only World Heritage site and was inscribed on the World Heritage List in 1996 under criteria VII, IX, and X, as it is the largest barrier reef in the northern hemisphere with a varied, unbroken ecosystem with a high level of biodiversity. However, due to mismanagement, the site was later placed on the List of World Heritage in Danger in 2009. This was due to a variety of issues, including the selling off of land within the boundaries of the site for hotel development, but it predominantly stemmed from the site's fragmented planning and management system, wherein NGOs were predominantly responsible for managing the site. According to UNESCO (2009), this forced some NGOs to turn to tourism to raise money for conservation activities, which, due to increased visitation and development, posed additional risks to the site. While these seem like insurmountable challenges, particularly as they require broad, government-level changes in policy planning, it is commendable how Belize strove to change direction.

In 2011, a National Sustainable Tourism Management Plan was developed for the entirety of Belize, which dictates tourism management and development up to 2030. When referring to the BBRRS, the focus has shifted to a conservation-driven approach, wherein "the main objective is to limit growth, only allowing it for necessary improvements to existing homes, resorts, lodges and other facilities" (Ministry of Tourism and Civil Aviation, 2012, p. 54). This was followed by the adoption of the Integrated Coastal Zone Management Plan in 2016, which developed a broad coastal management system that recognizes the variety of stakeholders, including local community actors and indigenous communities, involved in the management of the entirety of Belize's coastal system (CZMAI, 2016). The system also emphasizes, again, the importance of conservation in relation to the BBRRS World Heritage site. The final act that assisted in the removal of the BBRRS from the List of World Heritage in Danger was the banning of oil drilling within "the entire maritime zone of Belize" (UNESCO, 2018a). This concerted effort by the government of Belize resulted in the removal of the property from the Danger List at the 42nd committee meeting in 2018. In this instance, a clear dedication to the tenets of the World Heritage Convention and a willingness to enact sustainable management systems assisted in the amelioration of a severely degraded World Heritage site, highlighting the importance of management to the protection and conservation of sites.

Liburd and Becken (2017) caution against endangering the site's conservation, particularly as Outstanding Universal Value is less adaptable to change then normal values in protected areas. This can have repercussions, then, on other aspects of site management. For example, as protection and site preservation are the ultimate goal of the convention, educating people about the site through "presentation" is only acceptable when it is compatible with this guiding rationale (Buckley, 2018). However, preservation does not have to be confrontational to tourist preferences and values. As was seen in the work of Alazaizeh et al. (2016b, p. 156), visitors to Petra Archaeological Park in Jordan were found to value site preservation over use and wanted management to directly respond to issues. Thus although planning for tourism in order to preserve the site's Outstanding Universal Value can potentially be considered disruptive to tourist activity on-site, this does not imply that it would be seen negatively by visitors.

While the conceptualization of Outstanding Universal Value can, as Schmutz and Elliott (2017) indicated, be understood as a standardization mechanism, it can lead to the exclusion of practices that fall outside these heritage norms. This can cause problems at the local level, particularly when there are issues related to access to the required skill sets. However, even when these are solved, it is obvious that standardization falls short due to variations in local implementation (Elliott & Schmutz, 2016). Therefore, it is important to take into account traditional methods of preservation, although Chirikure et al. (2016) have highlighted that, in the case of Africa, there is a need to blend these traditions with modern, Western conservation practices in order to respond to the fluctuating post-colonial context. At the Cultural Landscape of Bali Province: The Subak System as a Manifestation of the Tri Hita Karana Philosophy site, the local community is responsible for general site management through the use of the existing traditional land management systems (Miura & Sarjana, 2016). However, it is not merely physical conservation that can be impacted by conflicts between UNESCO and the local context. In China, the heritage narrative of the West Lake World Heritage site was adapted to Western expectations in order to ensure its listing and please the external, international experts (Zhang, 2017). As can be seen, management should be about "creating a dialogue and documenting local management practices. If extended dialogue does not reveal a shared interest amongst stakeholders in World Heritage status, then nomination should not be pursued" (Human, 2015, p. 166).

While, ideally, Human's (2015) advice should be followed, this is not always the case, which often leads to significant friction among the various stakeholders at local level. This is visible in Hahoe Village, Korea, where growth in visitation has resulted in negative impacts on the site, with the local community highlighting problems with "traffic congestion, littering, noise pollution, overcrowding and invasion of privacy" (Kim, 2016, p. 10). In Malaysia, Melaka has witnessed a decrease in residents in the historic center due to an increase in tourism and a shift toward a tourism-focused local economy, which has caused rents to rise, forcing the local population to relocate (King, 2016). A similar situation can be seen in George Town, the second half of the World Heritage site of which Melaka is a part. Due to the emphasis on tourism combined with the removal of rent controls, individuals who had lived in the old city center were forced to relocate to more affordable areas, resulting in "gentrification" of the old town (Gin, 2016, pp. 188–189). This lack of access is not merely an aspect of urban World Heritage centers but can also be seen in more enclosed sites, notably through the institution of entry fees. These can occasionally be prohibitive for local populations resulting in their inability to access their own sites (Cochrane, 2016b). Furthermore, when visitor fees are lowered for domestic visitors, this can lead to disapproval by foreign tourists. This is particularly evident in Ghana at Cape Coast and Elmina Castles, where some African American tourists, who view the castles as the last place in Africa that their ancestors saw, object to paying a fee at all (Reed, 2015).

Even when there is a decent level of dialogue between the local stakeholders in regard to site management, local management issues can be exacerbated by bad on-site planning, often due to a focus on tourism growth as opposed to sustainability. This, combined with a growth in global tourist numbers, has caused many sites to exceed their carrying capacity, resulting in what is now being referred to as overtourism. While Venice has received significant media coverage due to the rising unrest in the face of this threat, other World Heritage sites have also been suffering. The historic center of Macau is currently facing heavy congestion due to a high proportion of short day trips lasting only several hours, with visitors clustered in a few specific key locations (Lee & Rii, 2016). Tourist visitation in Borobudur, located on Java in

Indonesia, is also not well managed, and heavy tourist numbers have caused damage to the site, particularly parts of the temples deemed to have "spiritual powers to which local guides like to draw attention" (Hitchcock & Putra, 2016). Exceeding carrying capacity can also be problematic for the tourists themselves, who indicate that overcrowding is a negative aspect of their visit. According to research undertaken by Alazaizeh et al. (2016a) at Petra Archaeological Park in Jordan, their segmented groups of tourists all indicated that higher numbers of visitors on-site were unacceptable but differed in terms of how many people could be in one place before it became "overcrowded." Luang Prabang was highlighted as being crowded but only negatively so during very specific sightseeing events – i.e., sunset in one location (Lenaertes, 2016). As can be seen, tourism planning is necessary to ensure sustainable outcomes (Job et al., 2017), particularly as overtourism negatively impacts all stakeholders as well as the World Heritage site itself.

As can be seen, a balance must be struck between preservation/conservation and use in order to avoid unnecessary damage due to overtourism. This requires that the management of tourism function in such a way that allows for visitation without undue damage thus protecting the site for future generations (Drost, 1996). There are some examples of successful collaborations, such as the more remote Swedish site, the Great Copper Mountain of Falun. There the World Heritage designation has sparked new collaborations, which in turn have led to better development of tourism on-site while simultaneously respecting the preservation requirements of UNESCO (Heldt Cassel & Pashkevich, 2014). However, there are instances where conservation may have gone too far. For example, the cultural World Heritage site of Ouadi Qadisha (the Holy Valley) and the Forest of the Cedars of God (Horsh Arz el-Rab) includes the remnants of an ancient cedar forest, and a visit to this site is highly structured in order to ensure the safety of the trees. This results in what Shackley (2005, p. 142) calls "a sterile tree museum." In some cases, though, minimal interventions are necessary in order to both conserve a site and provide a pleasant tourist experience. McGuiness et al. (2017) emphasize the importance of conducting research into tourist needs prior to commencing any alterations to the visitor experience, particularly as the visitors may be content with the current offering, however basic it may appear. As was noted in Chapter 2, tourist requirements can vary, and often simple things on-site are more important than a grand performance.

The management of tourism at the local level is especially important considering that the reasoning behind listing, particularly for less developed states, is often focused on economic gains, specifically through potential tourism increases, and thus tourism spending, in and around the site. Musitelli (2002, p. 327) highlights that "heritage has asserted itself in the course of the past two decades, as a recognized component of development. From now on heritage will be taken into account when anyone reflects on new strategies of development." The Organisation for Economic Co-operation and Development (OECD) (2009) has noted that culture has been adopted as a method of local regeneration in urban environments, which assists in reinvigorating the depressed local economic situation. In comparison, "in rural areas, tourism is used to support traditional livelihoods and crafts and sustain communities threatened with out-migration . . . Cultural tourism can be particularly important for rural areas, since there are often few alternative sources of income" (OECD, 2009, p. 24). It is unsurprising, then, that World Heritage as a development tool would be particularly attractive to States Parties on the lower end of the HDI that may also be especially interested in increasing their share of international tourism flows.

In fact, according to Leask (2006), two major implications of World Heritage site inscription relate to possible tourism gains and economic development. This is even more significant when considering that, per Frey and Steiner's (2010, p. 16) research, "the List tends to be beneficial where heritage sites are undetected, disregarded by national decision-makers, not commercially exploitable, and where there are inadequate national financial resources, political control and technical knowledge for conservation." Direct tourism flows to listed sites can be a boon to the local economy in developing countries, especially as heritage sites often attract foreign currency, which has led to "a scramble in [Less Developed Countries] to inscribe as many heritage sites as possible on UNESCO's World Heritage List" (Timothy & Nyaupane, 2009, p. 11). "Communities are often keen to present their World Heritage Sites to visitors or to exploit them as tourism resources in the anticipation of economic gain" (Millar, 2006, p. 51). However, the overemphasis on tourism may cause problems at the local level, particularly if tourists expect the quality of the tourism infrastructure to be equivalent to or better than that found in more developed countries, regardless of the actual financial situation within the host country (Cohen, 1972). Although a product of earlier travel trends, Cohen's (1972) work is still relevant in today's more specialized tourism environment. For example, the Chongoni Rock-Art Area in Malawi has been trying to construct an interpretation center in order to comply with their management plan. The center will be air-conditioned and include a café, bathroom facilities, and seating area for visitors to rest. This was deemed necessary in order to attract more international tourists to the site and is indicative of the type of burden that a site may face in a push to attract tourists.

When referring to less developed signatories to the World Heritage Convention, Ashworth and van der Aa (2006) specified that there is a greater emphasis on economic gains than on the actual purpose of the World

Heritage Convention: site preservation and conservation. Interestingly, Conradin and Wiesmann (2015, p. 699) found that World Heritage status at natural sites in the less developed world both assisted in improving conservation and helped to increase tourism at the site, which they suggest may be a result of the fact that the sites "are typically less developed" in comparison with those in more developed countries. They proposed that one of the reasons that the World Heritage status can be perceived as more valuable at lower levels of development is due to the difference in the way in which this status is understood between less and more developed states. "In the North, [World Natural Heritage] status is primarily understood as a reward for past conservation efforts. In the South, [World Natural Heritage] status is an aid to safeguarding some of the world's most significant natural habitats" (Conradin & Wiesmann, 2015, p. 698). It should be noted, though, that visitor fees, which are a common method used to ensure support for conservation activities, normally don't even cover daily operating costs let alone allow for serious investment in protection and conservation measures (Cochrane and Tapper, 2006). Thus, there needs to be an additional level of support for site protection in order to ensure that the economic injections into the site can also aid the development of the local community.

In certain instances, while tourism does, generally, promote economic growth, it is not substantial enough to promote a rapid advancement in terms of economic development. In Arezki et al.'s (2009, p. 16) research, "to reach growth of 6 percent per year, [a developing country] would need to increase tourism receipts as a share of exports more than 70%." Therefore, only a large growth in tourist visitation and spending could effectively trigger development. In contrast, VanBlarcom and Kayahan (2011) observed that, in the case of Canadian World Heritage proximity, small increases in tourism can have a significant impact on the local economy through the infusion of tourist cash into local small businesses. This highlights the problems identified by Su and Lin (2014) in regard to the use of tourism visitation data as a justification for potential economic development. They underscore that "a gap between tourist arrivals and tourist incomes may exist, because the consumption behavior of tourists may differ across countries" (Su & Lin, 2014, p. 57). In some cases, increased visitation can cause economic issues when monetary benefits, which are often the priority for regional and national governments, do not manifest themselves at sites. In Jimura's (2011) study of Ogimachi, Shirakawa, Japan, he found that while there was a significant increase in tourist visitation since inscription, the tourists spent little. Furthermore, as was seen in Buckley (2018, p. 9), "high visitor numbers [. . .] do not automatically create high impacts." Therefore, whether or not the World Heritage brand attracts tourists, as was discussed in Chapter 3, may be inconsequential in terms of predicting potential economic development from a World Heritage site.

Overall, while heritage tourism appears to be a panacea for struggling localities, many of the aspects highlighted by Frey and Steiner (2010), such as insufficient funding, political power, or conservation prowess, are also potential risks for localized World Heritage management. For example, Timothy and Nyaupane (2009, p. 64) found that "local residents often lack skills and investment abilities needed to establish tourism-related businesses and often end up with low-investment businesses and low-paying jobs." This can result in future benefits from heritage tourism being transferred outside of the local context, if not the national in certain instances where there is foreign control of the local tourism economy. The implication of non-acknowledgment of these risks was identified by Millar (2006, pp. 38–39), who remarked that

> in states with weak economies World Heritage Site status was eagerly sought as a kite mark for the promotion of mass tourism, under the guise of international cultural tourism, without any consideration as to whether the local people and local infrastructure had the capacity to respond effectively to the demands.

Additionally, the improvement of certain aspects may exacerbate others to the ultimate detriment of the site and local environs. For example, at Tubbataha Reefs Natural Park in the Philippines, the development of tourism infrastructure has sidelined the local population, who still lack full access even to electricity. Additionally, the tourists who benefit from this infrastructure tend to visit on prepaid trips, injecting little into the local economy (Fross, 2016).

While the previous conversation focusing on tourism-driven development has predominantly been about less developed countries, it should be noted that these effects could potentially also be seen in impoverished areas of developed countries given the importance of the local context. In Rodwell's (2002, pp. 57–58) analysis of five industrial heritage sites in the UK, all of the sites possessed management plans that were overly driven by tourism gains while being "too little focused on the role of heritage within the local community, too complacent in relation to the effectiveness of protective measures, and generally ignorant of the human aspect of cultural heritage." A similar situation was observed in Liverpool, which is currently on the List of World Heritage in Danger due to development planning pressures. However, within the debate surrounding this issue, the human element has been lost with "a few outspoken dominant parties forging an increasingly polarized debate pitting conservation and World Heritage against modern development" (Garcia et al., 2013, p. 21). As can be seen in these examples, as well as the previous presentation of place-specific management, people are often the catalyst for, as well as an obstacle to, sound site management, and they are at the core of good World Heritage governance.

People

The discussion on the planning and place-based aspects of World Heritage management has highlighted the significance of people to the entirety of the World Heritage management system. Consequently, it is fitting that UNESCO has recently shifted its focus toward a more participatory, multi-stakeholder approach with an emphasis on bottom-up management of World Heritage sites. This inclusionary process has worked well in some instances, as was observed in Vigan in the Philippines. There, the local community was actively involved in the development and planning process of the area's World Heritage–driven development (Akpedonu, 2016). An excellent example of World Heritage development that placed the local community at the forefront is visible in the case of Humayun's Tomb, found in Box 4.2.

In some instances, there may be higher levels of participation within a country context, based on the location of the communities. This was seen in Rasoolimanesh, Ringle et al. (2017) who found disparities between rural and urban residents in Malaysian World Heritage sites, wherein the local residents in urban George Town had higher levels of engagement in the tourism planning process in comparison with their rural counterparts in Lenggong. Furthermore, local inclusion does not always negate clashes between levels of management. In Bali, for example, local communities were not only actively involved in the planning process, but, as noted in the previous section, they are also directly responsible for the management of the cultural landscape (Miura & Sarjana, 2016). Interestingly, MacRae (2017) has indicated that local involvement has actually resulted in "friction" around site management, as there is a noted disconnect between the global and national plans and reality at the local level.

Box 4.2   Holistic integration of planning, place, and people: Humayun's Tomb, Delhi, India

Management of World Heritage sites and tourism requires the successful planning of management systems, which take into account local contexts and include local communities in the decision-making process. An excellent example of the development of this type of system was seen at Humayun's Tomb, which is a World Heritage site located in New Delhi, India. It was inscribed in 1993 under criteria II and IV, as it is an excellent grand scale example of a Mughal garden tomb and representative of the power of the Mughal rulers. The site itself had fallen into disrepair by the mid-2000s (AKTC, 2014), and, following a successful garden restoration project on-property by the Aga Khan Trust for Culture (AKTC), the Nizamuddin Urban

Renewal Initiative was officially inaugurated in 2007 through a memorandum of understanding, which formalized the development of a public-private partnership (AKDN, 2016b). The project was holistic in its approach, integrating conservation of the World Heritage site and surrounding heritage properties with local development through a community-driven approach (AKDN, 2016a). The successful design and implementation of the project relied on the AKTC working in tandem with government agencies, community and religious leaders, young people, vendors, and business, as well as both men and women from the local community (AKTC, 2014). This not only facilitated essential multi-stakeholder interworking but also ensured that the facilities that were created during the project are now managed by the local community (National Institute of Urban Affairs, 2015).

While the project included many development projects focused on the improvement of green spaces, better educational facilities, access to healthcare, and improvements to local infrastructure, several aspects specifically addressed the World Heritage site and tourism. An essential facet of the ten-year project was the restoration of Humayun's Tomb and the surrounding monuments. However, in order to ensure that this work benefited the local community, several young men from Nizamuddin Basti were trained in traditional tile making (AKDN, 2013) and sandstone craftsmanship, which would provide continuing employment past the end of the project (AKDN, 2008). Female community members, instead, were organized into cooperatives and trained in fabric-based crafts, including local embroidery techniques (*aari* and *zardozi*), and *sanjhi*, which is a traditional paper cutting craft (AKDN, 2015). These cooperatives have been very successful at selling their goods both at the World Heritage site and in other venues and, thus, have allowed women to contribute to their family's income, assisting in the overall amelioration of their situations. The final World Heritage tourism initiative involved the development of a heritage tour guide program, wherein local youth were trained to provide tours that not only showcase the World Heritage site but also the heritage within Nizamuddin Basti itself. This has been quite successful and again provided training to the local community, which allows them to continue to provide for themselves even after the project has finished. While this has been a very brief overview of an extremely intricate, decade-long project, it still illustrates the benefits that can be derived from World Heritage tourism when a holistic management system is well planned and takes into account the local context while undertaking a people-first management style.

While the example from Bali highlights problems related to the integration of various management structures, there are other issues that may arise when trying to increase local involvement in the management and planning process. For instance, there can be difficulties even in instances where significant community outreach has occurred, as was seen during the listing process of the Ningaloo Coast in Australia. In this case, there was visible community input into the planning process, but the local community still felt underrepresented and excluded, in part due to past experiences (Hughes et al., 2016). To avoid this situation, Hughes et al. (2016) stress the need for inclusive interactions across the board and not just in regard to World Heritage sites. Some problems may also arise due to a misinterpretation of exactly what local involvement within the World Heritage management process entails. This was observed in Turkey where "the primary strategy is to produce evidence of participation, rather than to substantively incorporate local communities into the management process" (Human, 2015, p. 173). It needs to be noted that, while active involvement in the planning process is preferred, exclusion does not necessarily preclude the local community from benefiting financially from the World Heritage site, most commonly in the form of heritage or natural tourism. For example, in a study on George Town in Malaysia, Rasoolimanesh, Jaafar et al. (2015) discovered that, even when local residents were pessimistic regarding World Heritage listing and subsequent tourism development, they still wanted to be a part of it in order to ensure that they also benefited financially. In fact, particularly in rural locations, economic involvement that leads to visible benefits for the local community can lead to increased optimism toward listing (Rasoolimanesh, Roldán et al., 2017).

This optimism needs to be tempered, however, as World Heritage is not always beneficial for local communities, particularly in the face of tourism development. At the Old Town of Lijiang site, this development has led to "the marginalization of the indigenous Naxi ethnic group, as a lot of local residents were coerced or forced to convert their homes into guesthouses, souvenir shops and other facilities for tourist consumption" (Chi et al., 2017, p. 210). In another example from China, the nomination and listing of Mount Sanqingshan National Park resulted in the formation of Yinhuwan Village as a result of the involuntary relocation of community members who had previously lived within the World Heritage area (Su et al., 2016). As a result, the villager's former, traditional occupations disappeared, and the newly formed community was provided with specific advantages that were designed to incentivize engagement in the tourism. This has resulted in their dependence on income from tourist activities, placing them at high risk from economic or political shifts (Su et al., 2016). However, this does not mean that these same communities are not active in the tourism system.

For example, according to research by Xiang and Wall (2015) villagers from Taqian, who were relocated, in line with government policy, from the Mount Taishan World Heritage site, were overwhelmingly positive toward tourism development and tourists themselves. According to Yan (2015), though, participation in tourist activities can be somewhat coerced as the Chinese government uses moralistic arguments around heritage in order to regulate the behavior of the local community.

It needs to be stated that, while there are many examples of local marginalization in China, this is not an exclusively Chinese activity. Many nations with traditional top-down government structures engage in the same actions. For instance, Mexico has a history of marginalization of Mayan ethnic groups while simultaneously benefiting from the use of their culture, notably in the marketing and management of tourism at Mayan World Heritage sites (Evans, 2005). In Levuka, Fiji, World Heritage site inscription was predominantly driven by the non-native Fijians, as ethnic Fijians were ambivalent, if not outright antagonistic, toward the site (Harrison, 2005). In Liverpool, Garcia et al. (2013, p. 37) noted that currently "the value generated by the World Heritage status is . . . concentrated disproportionately within the city centre, at the expense of the disenfranchised surround areas of the city." In certain cases, while a nod has been given to the bottom-up approach through local involvement in the nomination and management process, the final decisions disregard the needs of the local population in favor of national-level goals. This was observed at the Shirakami Sanchi World Heritage site in Japan. During the planning process, the government engaged with the local community, but the final decision prioritized preservation of the environment over local site use (Mason, 2015). It is precisely this situation that Theuma and Grima (2006) warn against when they emphasize the need to be cautious about prioritizing conservation to the extent that all of the site's use value held by a local community becomes dismissed as irrelevant.

While marginalization in World Heritage site planning and management processes has resulted in problems in certain states, further complications occur when this marginalization extends into eventual tourism development on-site, particularly in relation to the intangible heritage associated with the site. This is most common where there are disconnects between the dominant tourism-driven heritage narrative and that provided by the local community. This is visible at Angkor Wat in Cambodia where the current official discourse emphasizes the site's history, specifically placing it in an ancient historical context. This has resulted in policies that prioritize the conservation and preservation of this historic past, which in turn not only minimizes but also destroys the modern, living culture attached to the site by the Khmer people (Winter, 2005). It should be noted that, dependent on who controls the narrative, local populations can also fight against national or international heritage discourse. This can be seen at the Prambanan Temple Compounds site where the occurrence of several natural disasters resulted in UNESCO closing the site to visitation, instead providing a stand from which to view the site at a distance (Salazar, 2015). According to Salazar (2015, p. 127), this closure resulted in local guides, whose livelihoods were drastically affected due to the lack of tourism demand, reverting to local myths about the site and choosing to use "fewer references to [UNESCO] or to the officially sanctioned interpretation of the [World Heritage site]."

The complexities of intangible heritage and narrative construction are notable at sites that have contested or complicated histories and layered interpretations but are subject to official heritage narratives that are often state mandated as an attempt to develop a unified national identity within a diverse national environment. For example, according to King (2016), the official narrative in Melaka promotes the city as a multicultural symbol, a notable shift from the previous emphasis on Malay and Islamic heritage. However, on the ground, government bodies still underscore the importance of these histories to the detriment of local Chinese heritage. Lai and Ooi (2015) indicated that colonial, predominantly Christian, heritage is also sometimes seen as problematic. However, as these are important aspects of the World Heritage listing, one "response to the highly visible Portuguese past is to dilute its presence by asserting other histories" (Lai & Ooi, 2015, p. 287). These complex histories, however, can also play out when heritage tourism stakeholders are in control of the narrative. This is visible at Cape Coast and Elmina Castles in Ghana where there is an emphasis on the history of the slave trade, aimed in part at diasporic Africans (Reed, 2015). However, this is often prioritized over local narratives, which concentrate on the introduction of Christianity and the fight against colonialism, as well as historic use of the site as an area of recreation (Reed, 2015).

These studies illustrate the problematic nature of the World Heritage structure when applied to local areas with their own individual identities. According to Elliott and Schmutz (2012, p. 261), "by conceptualizing that diversity as part of a common (global) heritage, it also weakens the ontological primacy of particularized identities that were once the exclusive source of individual and group value." Thus, the creation of a unified narrative around the site can provide an additional layer of confusion to the visitor, especially if they are part of a marginalized group who recognize the site as their own. This throws light onto the issues caused by the universalist approach to listing, which can marginalize not only potential owners of the sites but also the visitors who may or may not have a cultural affinity to the site and their own narratives attached to it. However, Salazar (2014, p. 36) suggests that these tensions can be, at least partly, alleviated by "local heritage interpreters" who "play an instrumental role in mediating the tensions between on-going processes of global standardization and local differentiation." This further strengthens the importance of the local population as both custodians and champions of their own heritage in the face of growing standardization.

Marginalization of local voices does not always occur, however, and when local and official narratives coalesce, World Heritage status can be seen as a point of pride for local populations as well as a means to strengthen "international and national heritage identities" (Drost, 1996, p. 481). For example, in Hahoe Village in Korea, Kim (2016) noted that almost two-thirds of resident respondents were proud that their village had achieved World Heritage status. Pride of place was also seen in the case of Liverpool. Garcia et al. (2013, p. 14) found that the World Heritage listing "is a source of pride for many" but that

> some residents feel disengaged from the site due to its failure to encompass what they personally appreciate about the city's heritage; or because [World Heritage status] is seen to symbolize the neglect of their own neighbourhood at the expense of the city centre and other areas of the city.

Proximity to the site, therefore, appeared to result in a stronger sense of pride of place. In fact, according to Vong (2015), when heritage tourism is used to foster a sense of place identity, local communities feel pride toward their heritage, which in turn results in increased interest in conservation. However, it has been argued that as the List grows, the potential for the fostering of local pride will diminish due to the growing commonality of World Heritage (van der Aa et al., 2005).

While acknowledging narratives is an important step to integrating the local into the World Heritage management process, respectful practices are necessary, particularly in areas that have spiritual significance but also are being presented as tourist destinations. A good example of respectful practice can be seen in the recent shift in management at Uluru, also called Ayers Rock, in Australia. While the site was originally inscribed on the World Heritage List in 1987 under strictly natural criteria, the nomination was amended in 1994 to also include cultural criteria due to the site's significant spiritual importance for the aboriginal traditional owners, the Anangu. For the Anangu, climbing Uluru is an important spiritual task, which, although not expressly forbidden to tourists, is strongly discouraged. This can be seen as a spiritual/tourist use clash, as a large number of visitors will have come to Uluru specifically to undertake the climb (Shackley, 2006). In response to this issue, as well as the declining numbers of total climbs, both the Anangu and the National Park have chosen to end climbing officially on October 26, 2019 (Department of the Environment and Energy, 2017). While management of this site has obviously traditionally swung heavily in favor of tourist needs, the new trend toward respectful inclusion of spiritual norms is promising.

Not all examples of clashes have such positive outcomes. For example, a conflict of sacred and tourist needs is also visible at the Japanese World Heritage site Sacred Sites and Pilgrimage Routes in the Kii Mountain Range. Religious use of this site includes multiple pilgrimages to the remote shrines to illustrate knowledge of the trails in order to guide other pilgrims, but this has been compromised by the use of signage designed to guide tourists along these same routes (Jimura, 2016). In Luang Prabang, tourists did not always behave respectfully toward the monks and, during religious events, would not always follow protocol (Lenaertes, 2016). Additional issues can arise when tourists assign their own spiritual meanings where none exist among local communities or cultures. This is visible in Mesoamerican World Heritage sites such as Chichen Itza, which experienced a boom in "spiritual" tourists in 2012 who were preparing for the "Mayan" apocalypse. In Nigeria, the annual festival in the Osun-Osogbo Sacred Grove is a point of contention between local residents and tourists to the site. Woosnam et al. (2018, p. 144) note that a "healthy percentage" of the predominantly Christian and Muslim population view the event as a celebration of idolatry, although many acknowledge its importance as a preservation tool. However, in some cases, new spiritual use can be accepted by the site, as can be observed at Stonehenge, which has witnessed the rise of New Age druids who claim the stones as one of their holy sites. In this case, the new spiritual practitioners have even been granted access to perform their rituals on the solstice, imbuing the site with previously absent spiritual meaning.

As has been seen, people are essential to the management of World Heritage sites and World Heritage tourism. Local communities can assist in the management of the sites and help to develop a rich and distinct narrative for tourists. However, there have also been significant issues, particularly in areas where local input has not been requested or has been ignored. This is especially problematic as the inclusion of the local population is even more crucial when speaking of management from a tourism perspective. Support and buy-in by the local community is essential in order to ensure a pleasant tourist experience (Millar, 2006). Thus, though there has been some effort to integrate the local population into the World Heritage management process, the system's efforts are still falling short, especially when sidelining the local population has economic advantages. In order to create a more sustainable management system, there needs to be a concerted effort, at all levels of this system, to not only include the local stakeholders but also to actively listen without bias.

Conclusion

As has been seen throughout this chapter, it is essential to develop a fully integrated management system that takes into account the three themes of Planning, Place, and People. Planning is essential to the continuation of the entirety of the World Heritage system as well as to ensuring that there is a level of standardization in the implementation of management structures within the lower, more local system levels. It is at this point that the theme of Place intersects, as the application of World Heritage norms also requires a degree of negotiation in order to be accepted within the geographically specific context of individual World Heritage sites. This led to a discussion about the challenges associated with the implementation of sustainable tourism management plans, particularly in relation to the risks posed by overtourism and in balancing conservation and management. Additionally, there is a specific focus on World Heritage and tourism management in the context of international development, as there is a noted push to inscribe sites from less developed countries, specifically in the hope of raising their development levels. However, this often causes problems that eclipse any potential benefits of listing. The ramifications of this are often borne by the local community: the People. The final theme emphasized the importance of the local community within the World Heritage system and highlighted the benefits of including the local population in the World Heritage and tourism management process, as well as the problems that can appear when they are not given a seat at the table.

5   Current issues and future directions

Introduction

This work has sought to provide a broad overview of the relationship between UNESCO World Heritage and tourism through a holistic presentation of supply and demand. However, as has been seen, this relationship does not exist in a vacuum and is constantly impacted by external forces, many of which pose legitimate threats to World Heritage sites. This includes those problems that are the direct result of the tourism activity that takes place on-site. This chapter presents some of the specific threats faced by World Heritage sites today before discussing the largest threat to World Heritage, tourism, and humanity as a whole – global climate change. Increasingly, negative impacts from climate change have been identified as a rapidly approaching threat (IPCC, 2018), and this chapter highlights how this will affect World Heritage sites and tourism. Given how vulnerable these threats make World Heritage, it is necessary to highlight the inadequacies of the World Heritage system in its current form, particularly in regard to conservation issues. Finally, the chapter shifts into a discussion about the complexities involved in the relationship between World Heritage and tourism, and the suitability of tourism at World Heritage sites, particularly given the stated goals of the World Heritage Convention, is questioned.

Current threats to the World Heritage system

Regardless of all the care taken by the individual stakeholders at World Heritage sites, certain threats exist at a global level and can only be prevented through a concerted international effort. Many sites are threatened by a variety of human activities taking place on a global stage – i.e., war, political unrest, and terrorism. Past examples of terror incidents at World Heritage sites include the detonation of bombs in Borobudur in 1985 and the destruction of the Buddhas of Bamiyan by the Taliban in 2001, which were on the tentative list and were then inscribed to the World Heritage in Danger List in 2003. Recent threats can be seen in Syria where all six cultural sites (the Ancient City of Aleppo, the Ancient City of Bosra, the Ancient City of Damascus, the Ancient Villages of Northern Syria, the Crac des Chevaliers and Qal'at Salah El-Din, and the Site of Palmyra) were inscribed on the List of World Heritage in Danger at the 37th Committee meeting as a result of the civil war in the country and the direct threat to the sites themselves (UNESCO, 2013). These threats also pose a great risk to individual travelers, and, as is unsurprising, tourism to war-torn and violent areas of the world is highly discouraged. However, even in peaceful countries, the threat of terrorism can result in altered visitation experiences due to a potential terrorist threat. This was clearly visible at the Statue of Liberty post-9/11. According to Shackley (2006), when the site first reopened in 2004, visitors could only climb as far as the statue's pedestal and had to observe the interior of Lady Liberty through a glass plate. This restriction was removed in 2009 when the crown was reopened to the public, albeit in a strictly controlled manner.

Activities that are tied to global trade also pose a significant risk to World Heritage sites. This is visible in Phong Nha-Ke Bang National Park in Vietnam (Lien, 2016) and Sumatra (Cochrane, 2016a), which are facing threats from a variety of economically driven actions – i.e., poaching, mining, logging. While the previous examples can affect cultural sites, they are much more predominant at natural or mixed ones. On the other hand, natural sites are at a much lower risk of looting, which can be a significant problem at cultural and mixed World Heritage sites. Mackenzie and Davis (2014) detail a crime system that saw goods trafficked by looters at Cambodian heritage sites, including Angkor Wat and Sambor Prei Kuk, to international buyers, brokered through Thai intermediaries. Their study focuses on a historical analysis of this system, which was most active during the Cambodian Civil War (1970–1998), but, in the course of their research, one of the middlemen told them that, if they wanted a piece, looting and shipment could be arranged (Mackenzie & Davis, 2014). In comparison, looting activities at Petra in Jordan are more locally focused, with many of the stolen items available for sale to visitors around the site (Vella et al., 2015).

As can be seen at Petra, the global tourism market is a threat to World Heritage on a local level. This damage can be unintentional and/or the result of overtourism, which itself may be a consequence of heavy marketing. While marketing of World Heritage sites may generate an increase in visitation, if destinations aren't cautious, this can "lead to deterioration of the cultural and natural integrity of [World Heritage sites]" (Yang & Lin, 2014, p. 85). For example, increased visitation can cause specific conservation problems due to a higher level of foot traffic, which can cause a site, such as a fragile ecosystem or ancient cultural monument, to be damaged more quickly (Huang et al., 2012, Timothy & Nyaupane, 2009). At certain natural sites with highly vulnerable ecosystems, the presence of tourists in general can cause a myriad of problems. In a review of studies of the Wet Tropics World Heritage Area in Australia, Turton (2005, p. 144) found that

> while most visitor activities result in highly localized impacts at a small number of sites, threats such as the spread of weeds, feral animals and soil pathogens as a consequence of tourism and recreation activities potentially affect much larger areas.

In certain cases, improperly managed tourism can cause significant problems, both direct and indirect, as can be seen in the case of Lake Malawi in Box 5.1.

Box 5.1   Tourism as a threat: Lake Malawi, Malawi

Although tourism can bring potential economic benefits, when badly managed, it can cause significant issues for World Heritage sites, especially in relation to damage to a site's Outstanding Universal Value. This is visible at Lake Malawi, one of the largest freshwater lakes in Africa, which borders three separate countries: Tanzania, Malawi, and Mozambique. The largest part of the lake falls under Malawian territory, although a portion of it is part of a long-standing border dispute between Tanzania and Malawi. Lake Malawi National Park is a small, protected area of the lake found in the southern portion of the larger lake and located wholly within Malawi's national territory. The park was listed in 1984 under criteria VII, IX, and X for its "natural beauty," and as a microcosm of evolution and biodiversity (UNESCO, n.d.-a). According to the IUCN (2017), there are a multitude of activities currently threatening the World Heritage site. While industrial action, oil drilling in this case, as well as poaching activities pose a high threat to the site, Lake Malawi is an interesting case, as the two largest threats are the local community and tourism, which are, in themselves, interconnected. According to the State of Conservation Report (UNESCO, 2018b), the local population has more than doubled since the 1990s, which places significant stress on the local environment. This is visible in the current problems surrounding the growth in overfishing in the lake, the deforestation of the surrounding area for fuel wood, and increasing water pollution from sewage as well as small, badly maintained boats on the lake (IUCN, 2017).

Some of these issues are also caused by the tourism industry, for example, the release of sewage into the lake. The local community and tourists are also responsible for the increase of litter on-site, which is another significant threat. According to the IUCN (2017), tourism is also considered a threat in and of itself, particularly to the local fish population, as tourist activities place stress on its natural environment. Additionally, rapidly increasing tourist amenities have placed further strain on the local environment, which is already suffering due to the local population boom. As has been noted, tourism and the local community are interconnected, and, in terms of threats to the World Heritage site, perhaps the blame should be placed wholly on the tourism industry. Most local issues stem from a rapid increase in population, which is a direct result of the movement of non-locals to the area in order to work in the tourism industry (IUCN, 2017). Thus tourism, in this case, could be considered the largest overall threat to the site and needs to not only be properly managed but also potentially decreased in order to protect the site.

Unmanaged tourism growth can also result in an increase in litter on-site, air pollution, and problems with human waste management, as was seen in Chapter 4 (Hejazi, 2008; Timothy & Nyaupane, 2009). While the tourism threats presented so far have been indirect forms of damage caused by incorrectly managed visitor flows, tourists can also pose a more direct threat when engaging in deliberate acts of vandalism. This was the case at Petra where "in April 2013 [a] restored elephant head was severely damaged when visitors to the site repeatedly threw multiple stones at the artifact, smashing away the animal's trunk" (Vella et al., 2015, p. 232). In Vietnam, Lien (2016, p. 307) noted that graffiti appeared on the walls of caves in Phong Nha-Ke Bang and "valuable stone artefacts" were handled by visitors. Both of these activities could potentially have been prevented through better management structures, but it is unrealistic to expect the entirety of all World Heritage sites to be constantly monitored, especially given the sheer scale of certain sites. Overall, given the threats identified, it becomes clear that often the risks that are the direct result of visitation may outweigh any potential benefits that can be gained from the continuation or commencement of tourism activities.

While all of the previous threats endanger certain segments of the World Heritage List, they may be a higher risk for some sites than others. In comparison, climate change is an ever-present threat to all World Heritage sites, with natural sites at particular risk, especially given their fragile ecosystems. According to the Intergovernmental Panel on Climate Change (IPCC,

2018), an increase in 1.5°C will have devastating effects on global ecosystems as well as place stress on already fragile social environments. Global climate change, then, can be understood as the most pressing threat to World Heritage sites and, indeed, humanity in general. UNESCO (2015) is well aware of this threat, having incorporated it into the *Policy Document for the Integration of a Sustainable Development Perspective into the Processes of the World Heritage Convention.* States Parties are advised to

> reduce the vulnerability of World Heritage properties and their settings as well as promote the social and economic resilience of local and associated communities to disaster and climate change through structural and non-structural measures, including public awareness-raising, training and education. Structural measures, in particularly should not adversely affect the [Outstanding Universal Value] of World Heritage properties.
>
> (UNESCO, 2015, p. 5)

The stress on the protection of Outstanding Universal Value can be seen as extremely limiting, particularly if the only protection method that will save most of the sites involves sacrificing a key element. Furthermore, the advice is strongly reactive to climate change instead of proactively fighting against it.

The need to combat climate change at a global level is clear when presented with the sites that are currently under the greatest threat from climate change – namely, coral reefs. According to a recent report from UNESCO, all listed coral reefs are at risk of severe annual bleaching events within this century if global temperatures continue to rise (Heron et al., 2018). According to Heron et al.,

> maintaining the Outstanding Universal Value of World Heritage-listed coral reef properties will continue to require strong on-site management of pressures as well as national and/or regional enabling legislation to restore resilience and reduce local human stressors while climate stabilization occurs.
>
> (2018, p. 4)

They stress, though, that this will not solve the problem alone and adherence to the Paris Climate Agreement is "essential to secure a sustainable future for World Heritage-listed coral reefs" (Heron et al., 2018, p. 4). However, even when plans are developed to specifically combat the impacts of climate change and promote site-level resilience, there is no guarantee that they will be implemented properly. This was visible at the Great Barrier

Reef World Heritage Area where a plan was developed but political will was lacking, which has resulted in further deterioration (Hall et al., 2018). Furthermore, there may be little that can feasibly be done to protect the reefs if global warming itself is not controlled as the ever increasing global temperatures leave the reefs at increasingly high rates of not only degeneration but also total annihilation (Hoegh-Guldberg et al., 2018).

Although coral reefs may be the most publicly discussed World Heritage sites currently under threat from climate change, many around the world face worsening conditions. Coastal erosion and the growing threat of large coastal storms, with accompanying storm surges, pose a significant risk to many natural and cultural properties worldwide that are located along the coast. Examples of at-risk coastal sites include Rapa Nui National Park in Chile, better known as Easter Island, and Everglades National Park in the USA, which is currently on the List of World Heritage in Danger due to the high risk of climate change–related damage. Sea level rise is another major risk factor for coastal heritage. Based on estimates by Marzeion and Levermann (2014), a global increase of 1°C will leave 47 sites highly vulnerable to sea level rise, and this more than doubles when global warming rises to 2°C, with 110 sites at risk. Flooding is another problem faced by coastal sites, as well as those further inland, such as the Tower of London, which is at risk of tidal flooding from the Thames. Other sites are going to face desertification, heightened risk of wildfires, and longer and more drastic droughts. Furthermore, increasing global temperatures will also impact biodiversity, resulting in the loss or alteration of habitat and geographical shifting of species (Prideaux & Thompson, 2017).

According to Liburd and Becken (2017, p. 124), "the concept of stewardship thus puts emphasis on the people involved in conservation efforts, their personal values and dynamic interrelations." Therefore, stewardship can be used to ensure that World Heritage sites are more resilient to climate change, but this can only help to a certain extant given the potential mass scale of the increasingly worse climate change impacts. Perry (2011) stresses the need for better climate-based monitoring at the most vulnerable sites as well as actively managing change through adaptation of the local environment – i.e., removal of invasive species, expanding the buffer zone of the World Heritage site, translocation of at-risk species. However, as noted by Hall et al. (2016, p. 16), monitoring the effects of climate change requires sufficient funding without which "organisations may need to adopt different strategies to try and ensure the allocation of sufficient working budgets in the future." This may require "a re-framing of values and new forms of conservation a management" in order to "prevent compromise of World Heritage values" (Wardell-Johnson et al., 2015, p. 142). Similarly, Prideaux and Thompson (2017, p. 88) highlight the need for mitigating activities in order to increase the resiliency of natural sites, which include "adjustments to infrastructure to reduce pressure on the ecosystem, using increased entry fees as a rationing device to reduce demand or in some cases, closing protected areas to tourism." Tourists to areas requiring protection could also be diverted to alternative sites close to the fragile World Heritage Areas in order to avoid human disturbance of sites' ecosystems (Perry, 2011). Thus, in particularly vulnerable and predominantly natural sites, stakeholders need to be prepared for the possible failure of the tourism market, especially should sites' natural attributes disappear.

However, this line of thinking may cause a significant amount of conflict given that, although UNESCO was designed to protect heritage sites, World Heritage status is now more of "a marketing device than a protection approach" (Caust & Vecco, 2017, p. 8). As has been seen elsewhere in this work, there is a concerted effort by many nations to acquire World Heritage status in the hopes of increasing their share of the global tourism market. Ironically, the climate change risks faced by especially vulnerable sites will only be exacerbated by tourism, particularly given the industry's heavy resource consumption (Gössling & Peeters, 2015). Furthermore, for sites at high risk, the mere presence of tourists can add additional, unnecessary stress to local environments. However, in some cases, these issues are not addressed. For example, tourist operators at the Great Barrier Reef "believe that climate change stories in the media will 'scare away guests'" and thus are generally unwilling to discuss climate change with tourists, fearing negative word of mouth (Goldberg et al., 2018, p. 252). Ironically, the threat of climate change to the Great Barrier Reef has led to a rise in "last chance tourism," as was observed in Piggott-McKellar and McNamara (2017). This type of tourism was partly driven by a fear of the reef disappearing due to its ever-worsening health (Piggott-McKellar & McNamara, 2017). This puts further stress on the already hyperfragile marine ecosystem, creating an almost cyclical rhythm of human-driven destruction.

While tourists can worsen the impacts of climate change at World Heritage destinations, it will also directly affect tourism flows to and from certain destinations. Hoogendoorn and Fitchett (2018, p. 744) highlight that "due to the changes in the length and quality of climate-dependent tourism seasons, the competitive advantage of certain destinations will be altered, ultimately affecting the viability of tourism businesses globally." For African destinations, this will mean coping with increases in average temperatures above comfortable levels for tourists and alterations in precipitation resulting in potential water shortages and droughts (Hoogendoorn & Fitchett, 2018). Based on the findings of the IPCC (2018), global warming increases will have disproportionately negative impacts on populations in less developed countries. If global tourism patterns shift away from these regions due to inhospitable local climates or resource shortages, World Heritage tourism-dependent communities may suffer, particularly as less developed countries are often driven to inscribe World Heritage sites specifically for the potential benefits that may be derived from a growth in tourism. Therefore, the impact of climate change is not merely physical but also can be economic and/or social, especially when the local community relies on tourism in order to generate income.

Where do we go from here?

As has been seen, World Heritage sites are complex entities attracting a variety of visitors. They have a plethora of marketing styles, but it remains unclear as to whether they specifically function as tourist attractors. In order to both protect their Outstanding Universal Value and provide a satisfactory visitor experience, sites need to utilize well-honed and site-specific management plans. However, as has just been discussed, even if everything is done to perfection, there are increasing external threats that are difficult to control by any lone State Party. This is complicated by the continually expanding list and the miniscule World Heritage Fund budget. Endlessly increasing the list both dilutes its value (Fyall & Rakic, 2006; Logan, 2012; van der Aa et al., 2005) and limits the amount of conservation work that can actually be undertaken either directly by UNESCO or in collaboration with other organizations (Bertacchini & Saccone, 2012; Frey et al., 2013; Musitelli, 2002). Furthermore, according to van der Aa et al. (2005), the convention's promises regarding individual site protection being a global issue are a moot point, as nations are held responsible for the protection of sites within their political boundaries. Thus, there appears to be a high level of uncertainty involved in relation to the potential benefits of World Heritage listing, particularly as the risks are not manageable through the UNESCO system itself. This is further compounded by the current emphasis on tourism as a panacea for struggling World Heritage sites.

Several authors have highlighted the risks that the World Heritage List faces if sites that are not of the highest quality continue to be inscribed (Logan, 2012; Plets, 2015). This is grounded in the belief that World Heritage is a brand that needs to be protected in order to ensure the continued benefits from World Heritage tourism. This conceptualization has been disputed within this work as well as by the author previously (Adie et al., 2018). However, the general premise that overstretching the list is detrimental to the whole concept of World Heritage is absolutely correct. It is a logical fallacy to assume that all heritage that is of national importance is also meaningful for the rest of the world. As was noted in the introduction to this book, even after the launch of the Global Strategy, the list is still heavily dominated by European sites. While there is also a growing Asian presence on the list, this is predominantly driven by Chinese nominations with 20% of all current Asian World Heritage sites being located in China. These sites, in combination with those found in Japan, Australia, and India, account for approximately 50% of all sites in Asia and the Pacific. However, regardless of this growth, 7 of the 19 new sites inscribed in 2018 are found in Europe and a further 4 in Asia and the Pacific with only 1 in Africa, the least represented region on the list.

Currently, one of the major problems associated with the overall World Heritage system is related to the manner in which it exerts power. The World Heritage Convention, as has already been seen, is an international treaty but lacks an enforcement mechanism. Instead, it functions as soft law, wherein state sovereignty is paramount to the international regulations set down by UNESCO. Unfortunately, this system functions on good faith, assuming that the States Parties that sign the convention will follow its regulations and be vigilant toward safeguarding their sites' Outstanding Universal Value. This may have functioned in the early years of the World Heritage Committee when the system was predominantly run by "a cosmopolitan subset of normally often nationally oriented heritage experts" (Brumann, 2014), but, with the growth in prestige-driven and economically motivated clientelism, how well can an honor system truly work? In essence, although a state may violate the convention through mismanagement of its World Heritage sites, the only retribution that it may face from the World Heritage Committee is having its site placed on the List of World Heritage in Danger, or, at absolute worst, delisted (Meskell & Brumann, 2015). However, even then, the process is complex and fraught with game playing and disregard of expert recommendations.

Similar to the recommendations for inscription, Willems (2014, pp. 116–117) observed that even though "the Danger List is only a tool to rally international cooperation and support and not a punishment, the advice to include highly threatened sites in the World Heritage in Danger List has been mostly disregarded." This political maneuvering in order to prevent inscription on the List of World Heritage in Danger was visible in 2010 in relation to the Mapungubwe Cultural Landscape in South Africa (Bertacchini et al., 2017, Meskell, 2013). In this case, both the IUCN and ICO-MOS emphasized the threat of active coal mining occurring within the site's buffer zone, but Russia and India threw their support behind South Africa, resulting in a "BRICS alliance" (Bertacchini et al., 2017, p. 343). This halted the South African site's addition to the List of World Heritage in Danger. However, it also illustrated the level of deal making within the committee level, as, unsurprisingly, when the conservation levels of Russia's site, the Virgin Komi Forests, came into question later due to gold mining at the site, South Africa came to its aid (Bertacchini et al., 2017; Meskell, 2013). Given the rejection of expert opinion combined with backroom dealing, it has become clear that UNESCO's power to force States Parties to comply with conservation and protection standards through "shaming" activities is waning if not completely nonexistent.

Thus delisting is exceedingly rare, with only two deletions having occurred since the creation of the World Heritage List. This is due to the fact that the delisting process is onerous, as it provides ample time for the relevant States Parties to remedy the situation. Additionally, although a site may be struggling, delisting will only happen if one of two conditions is met, specifically:

a) where the property has deteriorated to the extent that it has lost those characteristics which determined its inclusion in the World Heritage List; and
b) where the intrinsic qualities of a World Heritage site were already threatened at the time of its nomination by human action and where the necessary corrective measures as outlined by the State Party at the time, have not been taken within the time proposed.

(UNESCO, 2017, p. 53)

However, even when a site is found to meet these criteria, the World Heritage Committee will still open a line of communication with the responsible State Party to try to address the issues threatening the site before any delisting action occurs. This is due to the fact that

> deletion of a site . . . raises the spectre of immediate disadvantages, such as a loss of national esteem from public exposure of poor con-duct, loss of visitor income to that site, and the weakening of political influence within national government structures . . . [T]he harmful consequences of deletion may also be more long term, impacting up-on the future interests of the State Party under the [World Heritage Convention].

(Goodwin, 2010, p. 308)

This, combined with the politicization of the World Heritage process, may explain why delisting has only occurred twice in the history of the Convention.

Given the current state of the World Heritage Committee and the manner in which power is being used, what is the alternative in this scenario? Is it the creation of a global heritage system that is based on hard law with legal sanctions for those who break the Convention? Certainly not, as this concentrates too much power in the hands of a few non-experts who, as already indicated,

are more interested in the economic benefits of listing than heritage protection. However, as has been observed, the current system is insufficient,
lacking both the power and financial resources to adequately protect even a
fraction of the current list. In order to avoid the shift toward hard law and the
need to actively police errant States Parties, the list in its current form needs
to be reconsidered. Sites need to be reevaluated in relation to their actual
significance and a cap needs to be placed on the total number of possible
World Heritage sites in order to ensure that all sites can receive adequate
protection. Alternatively, contributions to the World Heritage Fund need to
rise substantially, and control of the World Heritage Committee should be
returned to experts who can adequately distribute funding based on need
and not on political will. However, for any of this to happen, there needs to
be a reckoning among all World Heritage stakeholders regarding the actual
purpose of the World Heritage List.

It's complicated: the future of World Heritage and tourism

At this point, it is clear that the World Heritage List is nothing more than
a political tool being used by certain nations in an attempt to maintain or
attain greater geo-political dominance. Additionally, it is a continuation of
colonial conceptualizations of how to preserve and protect sites deemed
to be of heritage significance, which may be attributed to the problematic nature of the scientific and technical knowledge used being derived
almost entirely from the Western academic ethos (Elliott & Schmutz, 2016).
Without significant change, the list may very well have reached its zenith.
The problematic nature of the List is inevitably intertwined with a desire to
increase tourism, which, as has been seen throughout this book, results in a
complicated relationship between World Heritage and tourism. This is visible in Buckley (2018, p. 571), who stresses the inherent self-serving nature
of the tourism industry by noting that the only reason that they would have
an interest in conservation activities is if it would lead to an obvious benefit
for themselves. This self-interest is visible in Liburd and Becken's (2017)
study on the Great Barrier Reef World Heritage site. They noted that, while
members of the tourism industry "see themselves as the key stewards" of
the site, they also "began to distance themselves from environmental lobby
groups whose strong campaigns were perceived as 'damaging to our tourism industry,' according to an industry representative" (Liburd & Becken,
2017, p. 1731). Perhaps one of the most problematic aspects of the World
Heritage List and tourism is their co-dependency, regardless of the fact that
World Heritage functions within the public realm and the tourism industry
is predominantly private, with the marked exception of tourism in North
Korea. How altruistic can the tourism industry be when driven, generally,
by profit margins and increased returns? The answer is, sadly, not much.

This begs the question as to whether or not they should be connected at all. At its core, the World Heritage List was designed as a conservation and preservation mechanism that highlighted a site's importance to the world as a whole. It was never conceived as a tourist magnet, although several sites added in the early years of the list were already tourist hot spots (i.e. Yellowstone National Park, Kathmandu Valley, the Historic Centre of Rome). In fact, as has been seen, tourism can often be in direct opposition to the values of the convention when not strictly controlled, resulting in the damage and destruction of the very focal point of its activity. What then is the solution? Obviously, closing the sites to all visitors except a select few would be deemed as elitist, and opening them to everyone for free would result in irreparable damage, especially without a plan to control for carrying capacity and to enhance conservation and protective measures. While the tourism industry as a whole should remain private, tourism at World Heritage sites needs to be responsible in nature, focused on the holistic benefits to the visitor, environment, local population, and site itself. This is reflected in Kraak's (2017) work, where she stresses the importance of a human rights-based approach to World Heritage conservation and management while acknowledging the complexity of its implementation in contexts where human rights are a contentious issue. Regardless of the difficulty, though, responsible tourism is the only option if World Heritage sites are going to remain open to visitation.

In areas with a human population, a community-based tourism model, then, would be most appropriate, particularly where the emphasis is on sustainability and not on increased profit. In other words, to reference Marx, from each according to its ability, to each according to its needs. In practice, this should look similar to the work done by the Aga Khan Foundation in Delhi, India, at the site of Humayun's Tomb, which was discussed in Chapter 4. This project tackled not only the conservation and restoration of the World Heritage site but also the poverty, inequality, and lack of opportunity found in the neighborhood directly adjacent to the site (Adie, 2019). However, this case is unique in that it had at its disposal immense resources, both financial and personnel related. Therefore, there would need to be sufficient support from UNESCO in order to ensure that the tourism activities are benefiting local communities. Nonetheless, tourism cannot be the only economic activity in the community. It is not a panacea and should not be relied upon as a bandage for socioeconomic problems. Instead, a diversified local economy is the best option for long-term, sustainable development so long as it integrates the concepts of equality, justice, and agency. In areas where there is no local population, tourism should be strictly controlled, and, as Prideaux and Thompson (2017) have indicated, sites should be closed to the public where the damage they cause is unmitigable.

However, responsible tourism is difficult to implement in the current geo-political environment, particularly as the tourism industry is just that, an industry, with most tourism systems integrated into the global tourism marketplace. In our current neoliberal capitalist world, this automatically implies that the purpose of tourism is the maximization of assets for the stakeholders. This is inherently at odds with UNESCO's recent push toward sustainable tourism practices at World Heritage sites. There is no way to engage in responsible tourism planning practices if all that matters is profit. Furthermore, without any alterations in the World Heritage system itself, it is likely that this push for inscription based on the false assumption that it will bring in foreign capital will continue until the List is no longer perceived to be of value. However, this focus on profit-driven tourism growth raises additional ethical issues, particularly for tourism in less developed countries. Namely, in a world rife with inequality and suffering, it is almost unethical to continuously be diverting funding to protect, particularly cultural, heritage that is neither extraordinary nor essential and has been listed merely as the result of political maneuvering driven by alleged future tourism profits.

References

Aaker, J.L. (1999). The malleable self: The role of self-expression in persuasion. *Journal of Marketing Research*, 36(1), pp. 45–57.

Adie, B.A. (2017). Franchising our heritage: The UNESCO World Heritage brand. *Tourism Management Perspectives*, 24, pp. 48–53.

Adie, B.A. (2019). Urban renewal, cultural tourism, and community development: Sharia principles in a non-Islamic state. In C.M. Hall and G. Prayag (Eds.), *The Routledge Handbook of Halal Hospitality and Islamic Tourism* (forthcoming). Abingdon, UK: Routledge.

Adie, B.A. and Hall, C.M. (2017). Who visits World Heritage? A comparative analysis of three cultural sites. *Journal of Heritage Tourism*, 12(1), pp. 67–80.

Adie, B.A., Hall, C.M. and Prayag, G. (2018). World Heritage as a placebo brand: A comparative analysis of three sites and marketing implications. *Journal of Sustainable Tourism*, 26(3), pp. 399–415.

AKDN (2008). *Humayun's Tomb-Nizamuddin Basti-Sundar Nursery Urban Renewal Initiative Progress Report*. Available at: http://annualreport2015.nizamuddinrenewal.org/docs/Annual_Report_2008.pdf. [Accessed on 26 February 2019].

AKDN (2013). *Humayun's Tomb-Nizamuddin Basti-Sundar Nursery Urban Renewal Initiative Annual Report 2013*. Available at: http://annualreport2015.nizamuddinrenewal.org/docs/Annual_Report_2013.pdf. [Accessed on 26 February 2019].

AKDN (2015). *Nizamuddin Urban Renewal Initiative 2015 Annual Report*. Available at: http://annualreport2015.nizamuddinrenewal.org/docs/Annual_Report_2015.pdf. [Accessed on 26 February 2019].

AKDN (2016a). *Improving Lives through Culture*. Available at: www.akdn.org/publication/improving-lives-through-culture. [Accessed on 26 February 2019].

AKDN (2016b). *India: Cultural Development: Overview*. Available at: www.akdn.org/where-we-work/south-asia/india/cultural-development/cultural-development-overview. [Accessed on 26 February 2019].

Akpedonu, E. (2016). Lessons from Vigan: A comparative analysis of successful urban heritage rehabilitation. In V.T. King (Ed.), *UNESCO in Southeast Asia: World Heritage Sites in Comparative Perspective* (pp. 108–139). Copenhagen: NIAS.

AKTC (2014). *Humayun's Tomb: Sundar Nursery: Hazrat Nizamuddin Basti Urban Renewal Initiative: Culture as a Tool for Urban Development.* Available at: www.akdn.org/publication/humanyuns-tomb-culture-tool-urban-development. [Accessed on 26 February 2019].

Alazaizeh, M.M., Hallo, J.C., Backman, S.J., Norman, W.C. and Vogel, M.A. (2016a). Crowding standards at Petra Archaeological Park: A comparative study of McKercher's five types of heritage tourists. *Journal of Heritage Tourism,* 11(4), pp. 364–381.

Alazaizeh, M.M., Hallo, J.C., Backman, S.J., Norman, W.C. and Vogel, M.A. (2016b). Value orientations and heritage tourism management at Petra Archaeological Park, Jordan. *Tourism Management,* 57, pp. 149–158.

Arezki, R., Cherif, R. and Piotrowski, J. (2009). *Tourism Specialization and Economic Development: Evidence from the UNESCO World Heritage List.* IMF Working Paper. International Monetary Fund.

Ashworth, G.J. and van der Aa, B.J.M. (2006). Strategy and policy for the World Heritage Convention: Goals, practices and future solutions. In A. Leask and A. Fyall (Eds.), *Managing World Heritage Sites* (pp. 147–158). Oxford, UK: Butterworth-Heinemann.

Baker, M.J. and Cameron, E. (2008). Critical success factors in destination marketing. *Tourism and Hospitality Research,* 8(2), pp. 79–97.

Baral, N., Hazen, H. and Thapa, B. (2017). Visitor perceptions of World Heritage value at Sagarmatha (Mt. Everest) National Park, Nepal. *Journal of Sustainable Tourism,* 25(10), pp. 1494–1512.

Baral, N., Kaul, S., Heinen, J.T. and Som, B.A. (2017). Estimating the value of the World Heritage site designation: A case study from Sagarmatha (Mount Everest) National Park, Nepal. *Journal of Sustainable Tourism,* 25(12), pp. 1776–1791.

Berni, I. (2005). Verso la Cultura l'Italia Ostenta una "Attenzione Distratta": Siamo un Paese Fortunato ma non lo Meritiamo [In terms of culture, Italy flaunts a "Distracted Attention": We are a fortunate country but we do not deserve it]. *Siti,* 1(2), pp. 10–12.

Bertacchini, E., Liuzza, C. and Meskell, L. (2017). Shifting the balance of power in the UNESCO World Heritage Committee: An empirical assessment. *International Journal of Cultural Policy,* 23(3), pp. 331–351.

Bertacchini, E. and Saccone, D. (2012). Toward a political economy of World Heritage. *Journal of Cultural Economics,* 36(4), pp. 327–352.

Bigné, J.E., Sánchez, M.I. and Sánchez, J. (2001). Tourism image, evaluation variables and after purchase behaviour: Inter-relationship. *Tourism Management,* 22, pp. 607–616.

Blamey, R.K. and Braithwaite, V.A. (1997). A social values segmentation of the potential ecotourism market. *Journal of Sustainable Tourism,* 5(1), pp. 29–45.

Boggio, A. (2000). From protections to protection: Rethinking Italian cultural heritage policy. *Columbia-VLA Journal of Law & the Arts,* 24, pp. 269–286.

Borgarino, M.P., Della Torre, S., Gasparoli, P. and Ronchi, A.T. (2016). Crespi d'Adda, Italy: The management plan as an opportunity to deal with change. *The Historic Environment: Policy & Practice,* 7(2–3), pp. 151–163.

Boyd, S.W. and Timothy, D.J. (2006). Marketing issues and World Heritage sites. In A. Leask and A. Fyall (Eds.). *Managing World Heritage Sites* (pp. 55–68). Oxford: Butterworth-Heinemann.

Bramwell, B. and Lane, B. (2011). Critical research on the governance of tourism and sustainability. *Journal of Sustainable Tourism*, 19(4–5), pp. 411–421.

Brumann, C. (2014). Shifting tides of world-making in the UNESCO World Heritage Convention: Cosmopolitanisms colliding. *Ethnic and Racial Studies*, 37(12), pp. 2176–2192.

Buckley, R. (2002). *World Heritage Icon Value: Contribution of World Heritage Branding to Nature Tourism*. Canberra: Australian Heritage Commission.

Buckley, R. (2004). The effects of World Heritage listing on tourism to Australian national parks. *Journal of Sustainable Tourism*, 12(1), pp. 70–84.

Buckley, R. (2018). Tourism and natural World Heritage: A complicated relationship. *Journal of Travel Research*, 57(5), pp. 563–578.

Butzmann, E. and Job, H. (2017). Developing a typology of sustainable protected area tourism products. *Journal of Sustainable Tourism*, 25(12), pp. 1736–1755.

Caldwell, N. and Freire, J.R. (2004). The differences between branding a country, a region and a city: Applying the brand box model. *Journal of Brand Management*, 12(1), pp. 50–61.

Caust, J. and Vecco, M. (2017). Is UNESCO World Heritage recognition a blessing or burden? Evidence from developing Asian countries. *Journal of Cultural Heritage*, 27, pp. 1–9.

Cellini, R. (2011). Is UNESCO recognition effective in fostering tourism? A comment on Yang, Lin and Han. *Tourism Management*, 32, pp. 452–454.

Chandler, J.A. and Costello, C.A. (2002). A profile of visitors at heritage tourism destinations in East Tennessee according to Plog's lifestyle activity level preferences model. *Journal of Travel Research*, 41, pp. 161–166.

Chi, C.G.-Q., Cai, R. and Li, Y. (2017). Factors influencing residents' subjective well-being at World Heritage sites. *Tourism Management*, 63, pp. 209–222.

Chikuta, O., du Plessis, E. and Saayman, M. (2019). Accessibility expectations of tourists with disabilities in national parks. *Tourism Planning & Development*, 16(1), pp. 75–92.

Chirikure, S., Mukwende, T. and Taruvinga, P. (2016). Post-colonial heritage conservation in Africa: Perspectives from drystone wall restorations at Khami World Heritage site, Zimbabwe. *International Journal of Heritage Studies*, 22(2), pp. 165–178.

Clarke, J. (2000). Tourism brands: An exploratory study of the brands box model. *Journal of Vacation Marketing*, 6(4), pp. 329–345.

Coastal Zone Management Authority and Institute (CZMAI). (2016). *Belize Integrated Coastal Zone Management Plan*. Belize City: CZMAI.

Cochrane, J. (2016a). It's a jungle out there: Contestation and conflict at Indonesia's natural World Heritage sites. In V.T. King (Ed.), *UNESCO in Southeast Asia: World Heritage Sites in Comparative Perspective* (pp. 313–346). Copenhagen: NIAS.

Cochrane, J. (2016b). Selling nature: Arrangements for tourism in Malaysia's natural World Heritage sites. In V.T. King (Ed.), *UNESCO in Southeast Asia: World Heritage Sites in Comparative Perspective* (pp. 367–378). Copenhagen: NIAS.

Cochrane, J. and Tapper, R. (2006). Tourism's contribution to World Heritage site management. In A. Leask and A. Fyall (Eds.), *Managing World Heritage Sites* (pp. 97–109). Oxford: Butterworth-Heinemann.

Cohen, E. (1972). Towards a sociology of international tourism. *Social Research*, 39(1), pp. 164–182.

Conradin, K. and Wiesmann, U. (2015). Protecting the South: Promoting the North? World Natural Heritage status in the global North and South. *Society and Natural Resources*, 28, pp. 689–702.

Crawford, K.R. (2015). Expectations and experiences of visitors at Giant's Causeway World Heritage site, Northern Ireland. In L. Bourdeau, M. Gravari-Barbas, and M. Robinson (Eds.), *World Heritage, Tourism and Identity: Inscription and Co-Production* (pp. 187–198). Burlington, VT: Ashgate Publishing Company.

Cuccia, T., Guccio, C. and Rizzo, I. (2016). The effects of UNESCO World Heritage list inscription on tourism destinations performance in Italian regions. *Economic Modelling*, 53, pp. 494–508.

Cutler, S.Q., Doherty, S. and Carmichael, B. (2015). Immediacy, photography and memory: The tourist experience of Machu Pichu. In L. Bourdeau, M. Gravari-Barbas, and M. Robinson (Eds.), *World Heritage, Tourism and Identity: Inscription and Co-Production* (pp. 131–145). Burlington, VT: Ashgate Publishing Company.

de Chernatony, L. and McWilliam, G. (1989). The strategic implications of clarifying how marketers interpret "brands." *Journal of Marketing Management*, 5(2), pp. 153–171.

Department of the Environment and Energy, Australian Government (2017). *Uluru Climb to Close*. Available at: www.environment.gov.au/mediarelease/uluru-climb-close. [Accessed on 15 November 2018].

Dewar, K., du Cros, H. and Li, W. (2012). The search for World Heritage brand awareness beyond the iconic heritage: A case study of the historic centre of Macao. *Journal of Heritage Tourism*, 7(4), pp. 323–339.

Di Giovine, M.A. (2009). *The Heritage-scape: UNESCO, World Heritage, and Tourism*. Lanham, MD: Lexington Books.

Drost, A. (1996). Developing sustainable tourism for World Heritage sites. *Annals of Tourism Research*, 23(2), pp. 479–492.

Elliott, M.A. and Schmutz, V. (2012). World Heritage: Constructing a universal cultural order. *Poetics*, 40, pp. 256–277.

Elliott, M.A. and Schmutz, V. (2016). Diffusion and decoupling in the World Heritage movement: Exploring global/local tensions in Africa. *European Journal of Cultural and Political Sociology*, 3(2–3), pp. 152–176.

Elmi, M. and Hinna, A. (2017). Global cultural policies and their management: The case of Italian UNESCO World Heritage sites. In T.R. Klassen, D. Cepiku, and T.J. Lah (Eds.), *The Routledge Handbook of Global Public Policy and Administration* (pp. 241–252). Abingdon, UK: Routledge.

Esparon, M., Stoeckl, N., Farr, M. and Larson, S. (2015). The significance of environmental values for destination competitiveness and sustainable tourism strategy making: Insights from Australia's Great Barrier Reef World Heritage area. *Journal of Sustainable Tourism*, 23(5), pp. 706–725.

Evans, G. (2005). Mundo Maya: From Cancún to city of culture: World Heritage in post-colonial Mesoamerica. In D. Harrison and M. Hitchcock (Eds.), *The Politics of World Heritage: Negotiating Tourism and Conservation* (pp. 35–49). Clevedon, UK: Channel View.

Francioni, F. (2008). The preamble. In F. Francioni (Ed.), *The 1972 World Heritage Convention: A Commentary* (pp. 11–21). Oxford: Oxford University Press.

Francioni, F. and Lenzerini, F. (2008). The future of the World Heritage Convention: Problems and prospects. In F. Francioni (Ed.), *The 1972 World Heritage Convention: A Commentary* (pp. 401–410). Oxford: Oxford University Press.

Freimund, W., Patterson, M., Bosak, K. and Saxen, S.W. (2009). *Final Report: Winter Experiences of Old Faithful Visitors in Yellowstone National Park*. Submitted by University of Montana, Department of Society and Conservation.

Frey, B.S., Pamini, P. and Steiner, L. (2013). Explaining the World Heritage list: An empirical study. *International Review of Economics*, 60, pp. 1–19.

Frey, B.S. and Steiner, L. (2010). World Heritage list: Does it make sense? *Center for Research in Economics, Management and the Arts*. Working Paper No. 2010–11, pp. 1–19.

Fross, J.K. (2016). Natural World Heritage sites and local communities: A conflict of interest? Two case studies from Palawan, the Philippines. In V.T. King (Ed.), *UNESCO in Southeast Asia: World Heritage Sites in Comparative Perspective* (pp. 347–366). Copenhagen: NIAS.

Fyall, A. and Rakic, T. (2006). The future market for World Heritage sites. In A. Leask and A. Fyall (Eds.), *Managing World Heritage Sites* (pp. 159–175). Oxford: Butterworth-Heinemann.

Galera, S. (2016). The benefits of legal globalization: Soft law: A case study of heritage law. *The Historic Environment: Policy & Practice*, 7(2–3), 237–247.

Garcia, B., Armitage, N. and Crone, S. (2013). *Heritage, Pride and Place: Exploring the Contribution of World Heritage Site Status to Liverpool's Sense of Place and Future Development: Final Report*. Institute of Cultural Capital.

Gin, O.K. (2016). Maverick George Town, Penang: Colonial outpost to a World Heritage site. In V.T. King (Ed.), *UNESCO in Southeast Asia: World Heritage Sites in Comparative Perspective* (pp. 169–197). Copenhagen: NIAS.

Goldberg, J., Birtles, A., Marshall, N., Curnock, M., Case, P. and Beeden, R. (2018). The role of Great Barrier Reef tourism operators in addressing climate change through strategic communication and direct action. *Journal of Sustainable Tourism*, 26(2), pp. 238–256.

Goodwin, E.J. (2010). The consequences of deleting World Heritage sites. *King's Law Journal*, 21, pp. 283–309.

Gössling, S. and Peeters, P. (2015). Assessing tourism's global environmental impact 1900–2050. *Journal of Sustainable Tourism*, 23(5), pp. 639–659.

Govers, R. and Go, F. (2009). *Place Branding: Glocal, Virtual and Physical Identities, Constructed Imagined and Experienced*. London: Palgrave Macmillan.

Guardian (2019, January 1). "It's a free-for-all": Shutdown brings turmoil to beloved US national parks. *The Guardian*, [online]. Available at: www.theguardian.com/environment/2018/dec/31/national-parks-shutdown-impact-joshua-tree-yosemite-yellowstone. [Accessed on 28 February 2019].

Hakala, U., Lätti, S. and Sandberg, B. (2011). Operationalising brand heritage and cultural heritage. *Journal of Product & Brand Management*, 20(6), pp. 447–456.

Hall, C.M. (2008). *Tourism Planning: Policies, Processes and Relationships* (2nd ed.). Essex, UK: Pearson Education Limited.

Hall, C.M. (2011). A typology of governance and its implications for tourism policy analysis. *Journal of Sustainable Tourism*, 19(4–5), pp. 437–457.

Hall, C.M., Baird, T., James, M. and Ram, Y. (2016). Climate change and cultural heritage: Conservation and heritage tourism in the Anthropocene. *Journal of Heritage Tourism*, 11(1), pp. 10–24.

Hall, C.M. and Piggin, R. (2001). Tourism and World Heritage in OECD countries. *Tourism Recreation Research*, 26(1), pp. 103–105.

Hall, C.M. and Piggin, R. (2002). Tourism business knowledge of World Heritage sites: A New Zealand case study. *International Journal of Tourism Research*, 4(5), pp. 401–411.

Hall, C.M. and Piggin, R. (2003). World Heritage sites: Managing the brand. In A. Fyall, B. Garrod, and A. Leask (Eds.), *Managing Visitor Attractions: New Directions* (pp. 203–219). Oxford: Butterworth-Heinemann.

Hall, C.M., Prayag, G. and Amore, A. (2018). *Tourism and Resilience: Individual, Organisational and Destination Perspectives*. Bristol, UK: Channel View Publications.

Halpenny, E.A., Arellano, A. and Stuart, S.A. (2015). The use and impact of World Heritage designation by Canadian heritage sites: An exploratory media analysis. In L. Bourdeau, M. Gravari-Barbas, and M. Robinson (Eds.), *World Heritage, Tourism and Identity: Inscription and Co-Production* (pp. 25–36). Burlington, VT: Ashgate Publishing Company.

Hardiman, N. and Burgin, S. (2013). World Heritage area listing of the Greater Blue Mountains-did it make a difference to visitation? *Tourism Management Perspectives*, 6, pp. 63–64.

Harrison, D. (2005). Levuka, Fiji: Contested heritage? In D. Harrison and M. Hitchcock (Eds.), *The Politics of World Heritage: Negotiating Tourism and Conservation* (pp. 66–89). Clevedon, UK: Channel View.

Hazen, H. (2008). "Of outstanding universal value": The challenge of scale in applying the World Heritage Convention at national parks in the US. *Geoforum*, 39, pp. 252–264.

Hazen, H. (2009). Valuing natural heritage: Park visitors' values related to World Heritage sites in the USA. *Current Issues in Tourism*, 12(2), pp. 165–181.

Healey, P. (2006). *Collaborative Planning: Shaping Places in Fragmented Societies* (2nd ed.). New York: Palgrave Macmillan.

Hejazi, M. (2008). The risks to cultural heritage in Western and Central Asia. *Journal of Asian Architecture and Building Engineering*, 7(2), pp. 239–245.

Heldt Cassel, S. and Pashkevich, A. (2014). World Heritage and tourism innovation: Institutional frameworks and local adaptation. *European Planning Studies*, 22(8), pp. 1625–1640.

Heron, S.F., van Hooidonk, R., Maynard, J., Anderson, K., Day, J.C., Hoegh-Guldberg, O., . . . Eakin, C.M. (2018). *Impacts of Climate Change on World Heritage Coral Reefs: Update to the First Global Scientific Assessment*. Paris: UNESCO World Heritage Centre.

Heslinga, J., Groote, P. and Vanclay, F. (2017). Strengthening governance processes to improve benefit-sharing from tourism in protected areas by using stakeholder analysis. *Journal of Sustainable Tourism*, pp. 1–15. https://doi.org/10.1080/0966 9582.2017.1408635

Hitchcock, M. and Putra, I.N.D. (2016). Prambanan and borobudur: Managing tourism and conservation in Indonesia. In V.T. King (Ed.), *UNESCO in Southeast Asia: World Heritage Sites in Comparative Perspective* (pp. 258–273). Copenhagen: NIAS.

Hoegh-Guldberg, O., Jacob, D., Taylor, M., Bindi, M., Brown, S., Camilloni, I., . . . Zhou, G. (2018). Impacts of 1.5°C global warming on natural and human systems. In V. Masson-Delmotte, P. Zhai, H.-O. Pörtner, D. Roberts, J. Skea, P.R. Shukla, A. Pirani, W. Moufouma-Okia, C. Péan, R. Pidcock, S. Connors, J.B.R. Matthews, Y. Chen, X. Zhou, M.I. Gomis, E. Lonnoy, T. Maycock, M. Tignor, and T. Waterfield (Eds.), *Global warming of 1.5°C: An IPCC Special Report on the Impacts of Global Warming of 1.5°C above Pre-Industrial Levels and Related Global Greenhouse Gas Emission Pathways, in the Context of Strengthening the Global Response to the Threat of Climate Change, Sustainable Development, and Efforts to Eradicate Poverty* [In Press].

Hoogendoorn, G. and Fitchett, J.M. (2018). Tourism and climate change: A review of threats and adaptation strategies for Africa. *Current Issues in Tourism*, 21(7), pp. 742–759.

Huang, C.-H., Tsaur, J.-R. and Yang, C.-H. (2012). Does the World Heritage list really induce more tourists? Evidence from Macau. *Tourism Management*, 33, pp. 1450–1457.

Hughes, M., Jones, T. and Phau, I. (2016). Community perceptions of a World Heritage nomination process: The ningaloo coast region of Western Australia. *Coastal Management*, 44(2), pp. 139–155.

Huh, J., Uysal, M. and McCleary, K. (2006). Cultural/heritage destinations: Tourist satisfaction and market segmentation. *Journal of Hospitality & Leisure Marketing*, 14(3), pp. 81–99.

Human, H. (2015). Democratising World Heritage: The policies and practices of community involvement in Turkey. *Journal of Social Archaeology*, 15(2), pp. 160–183.

Hvenegaard, G.T. (2002). Using tourist typologies for ecotourism research. *Journal of Ecotourism*, 1(1), pp. 7–18.

ICOMOS (1994). *The Nara Document on Authenticity*. Available at: www.icomos. org/charters/nara-e.pdf. [Accessed on 22 February 2019].

IPCC (2018). Summary for policymakers. In V. Masson-Delmotte, P. Zhai, H.-O. Pörtner, D. Roberts, J. Skea, P.R. Shukla, A. Pirani, W. Moufouma-Okia, C. Péan, R. Pidcock, S. Connors, J.B.R. Matthews, Y. Chen, X. Zhou, M.I. Gomis, E. Lonnoy, Maycock, M. Tignor, and T. Waterfield (Eds.), *Global Warming of 1.5°C: An IPCC Special Report on the Impacts of Global Warming of 1.5°C above Pre-Industrial Levels and Related Global Rreenhouse Gas Emission Pathways, in the Context of Strengthening the Global Response to the Threat of Climate Change, Sustainable Development, and Efforts to Eradicate Poverty* (pp. 1–32). Geneva, Switzerland: World Meteorological Organization.

IUCN (2017). *Lake Malawi National Park*. Available at: www.worldheritageoutlook. iucn.org/explore-sites/wdpaid/10904. [Accessed on 25 February 2019].

Jaafar, M., Noor, S.M. and Rasoolimanesh, S.M. (2015). Perception of local residents towards sustainable conservation programmes: A case study of the Lenggong World Cultural Heritage site. *Tourism Management*, 48, pp. 154–163.

James, L. and Winter, T. (2017). Expertise and the making of World Heritage policy. *International Journal of Cultural Policy*, 23(1), pp. 36–51.

Jansen-Verbeke, M. and McKercher, B. (2010). The tourism destiny of World Heritage cultural sites. In D.G. Pearce and R. Butler (Eds.), *Tourism Research: A 20–20 Vision* (pp. 190–202). Oxford: Goodfellow Publishers.

Jessop, B. (2011). Metagovernance. In M. Bevir (Ed.), *The Sage Handbook of Governance* (pp. 106–123). London: Sage Publications Ltd.

Jimura, T. (2011). The impact of World Heritage site designation on local communities: A study of Ogimachi, Shirakawa-mura, Japan. *Tourism Management*, 32, pp. 288–296.

Jimura, T. (2016). World Heritage site management: A case study of sacred sites and pilgrimage routes in the Kii mountain range, Japan. *Journal of Heritage Tourism*, 11(4), pp. 382–394.

Job, H., Becken, S. and Lane, B. (2017). Protected Ares in a neoliberal world and the role of tourism in supporting conservation and sustainable development: An assessment of strategic planning, zoning, impact monitoring, and tourism management at natural World Heritage sites. *Journal of Sustainable Tourism*, 25(12), pp. 1697–1718.

Jones, T.E., Yang, Y. and Yamamoto, K. (2017). Assessing the recreational value of World Heritage site inscription: A longitudinal travel cost analysis of Mount Fuji climbers. *Tourism Management*, 60, pp. 67–78.

Keller, K.L. and Lehmann, D.R. (2006). Brands and branding: Research findings and future priorities. *Marketing Science*, 25(6), pp. 740–759.

Kerstetter, D.L., Confer, J.J. and Graefe, A.R. (2001). An exploration of the specialization concept within the context of heritage tourism. *Journal of Travel Research*, 39, pp. 267–274.

Kim, H., Cheng, C.-K. and O'Leary, J.T. (2007). Understanding participation patterns and trends in tourism cultural attractions. *Tourism Management*, 28, pp. 1366–1371.

Kim, H., Oh, C.-O., Lee, S. and Lee, S. (2018). Assessing the economic values of World Heritage sites and the effects of perceived authenticity on their values. *International Journal of Tourism Research*, 20, pp. 126–136.

Kim, S. (2016). World Heritage site designation impacts on a historic village: A case study on residents' perceptions of Hahoe Village (Korea). *Sustainability*, 8(3), pp. 1–16.

King, L.M. and Halpenny, E.A. (2014). Communicating the World Heritage brand: Visitor awareness of UNESCO's World Heritage symbol and the implications for sites, stakeholders and sustainable management. *Journal of Sustainable Tourism*, 22(5), pp. 768–786.

King, L.M. and Prideaux, B. (2010). Special interest tourists collecting places and destinations: A case study of Australian World Heritage sites. *Journal of Vacation Marketing*, 16(3), pp. 235–247.

King, V.T. (2016). Melaka as a World Heritage site: Melaka as Malaysia? In V.T. King (Ed.), *UNESCO in Southeast Asia: World Heritage Sites in Comparative Perspective* (pp. 140–168). Copenhagen: NIAS.

Kraak, A.L. (2017). Impediments to a human rights-based approach to heritage conservation: The case of Bagan, Myanmar. *International Journal of Cultural Policy*, 23(4), pp. 433–445.

Kruger, M., Viljoen, A. and Saayman, M. (2017). Who visits the Kruger National Park, and why? Identifying target markets. *Journal of Travel & Tourism Marketing*, 34(3), pp. 312–340.

Lai, S. and Ooi, C.-S. (2015). Branded as a World Heritage city: The politics afterwards. *Place Branding and Public Diplomacy*, 11, pp. 276–292.

Lake District National Park Authority (2018). *World Heritage Site Brand Launched Today at Westmorland County Show*. Available at: www.lakedistrict.gov.uk/aboutus/media-centre/latest-news/news-releases/world-heritage-site-brand-launched-today-at-westmorland-county-show. [Accessed on 25 February 2019].

Lake District National Park Partnership (2019a). *FAQS*. Available at: http://lakesworldheritage.co.uk/faqs/. [Accessed on 25 February 2019].

Lake District National Park Partnership (2019b). *Marketing Toolkit: English Lake District World Heritage Site*. Available at: http://lakesworldheritage.co.uk/toolkit/. [Accessed on 25 February 2019].

Leask, A. (2006). World Heritage site designation. In A. Leask and A. Fyall (Eds.), *Managing World Heritage Sites* (pp. 5–19). Oxford: Butterworth-Heinemann.

Lee, E. (2010). World Heritage site status: Boon or bane? *The Newsletter*, 54, pp. 6–9.

Lee, M.Y. and Rii, H.U. (2016). An application of the vicious circle schema to the World Heritage site of Macau. *Journal of Heritage Tourism*, 11(2), pp. 126–142.

Lee, S., Phau, I. and Quintal, V. (2018). Exploring the effects of a "new" listing of a UNESCO World Heritage site: The case of Singapore Botanic Gardens. *Journal of Heritage Tourism*, 13(4), pp. 339–355.

Leiper, N. (1990). Tourist attraction systems. *Annals of Tourism Research*, 17(3), pp. 367–384.

Lenaertes, S. (2016). Visitor experience and interpretation at Luang Prabang World Heritage site. In V.T. King (Ed.), *UNESCO in Southeast Asia: World Heritage Sites in Comparative Perspective* (pp. 54–74). Copenhagen: NIAS.

Lew, A. and McKercher, B. (2006). Modeling tourist movements: A local destination analysis. *Annals of Tourism Research*, 33(2), pp. 403–423.

Liburd, J.J. and Becken, S. (2017). Values in nature conservation, tourism and UNESCO World Heritage site stewardship. *Journal of Sustainable Tourism*, 25(12), pp. 1719–1735.

Lien, V.H. (2016). From Ho Chi Minh Trail to World Heritage: The Phong Nha-Ke Bang nature reserve of Vietnam. In V.T. King (Ed.), *UNESCO in Southeast Asia: World Heritage Sites in Comparative Perspective* (pp. 291–312). Copenhagen: NIAS.

Light, D. and Prentice, R.C. (1994). Who consumes the heritage product? Implications for European heritage tourism. In G.J. Ashworth and P.J. Larkham (Eds.), *Building a New Heritage: Tourism, Culture and Identity in the New Europe* (pp. 90–116). London: Routledge.

Lloyd, D., Gilmour, S. and Stimpson, K. (2015). Promoting the Greater Blue Mountains World Heritage area: Environmental presentation within tourist brochures. *Journal of Heritage Tourism*, 10(4), pp. 325–344.

Logan, W. (2012). States, governance and the politics of culture: World Heritage in Asia. In P. Daly and T. Winter (Eds.), *Routledge Handbook of Heritage in Asia* (pp. 113–128). Abingdon, UK: Routledge.

Lo Piccolo, F., Leone, D. and Pizzuto, P. (2012). The (controversial) role of the UNESCO WHL management plans in promoting sustainable tourism development. *Journal of Policy Research in Tourism, Leisure and Events*, 4(3), pp. 249–276.

MacKenzie, S. and Davis, T. (2014). Temple looting in Cambodia: Anatomy of a statue trafficking network. *British Journal of Criminology*, 54, pp. 722–740.

MacRae, G. (2017). Universal heritage meets local livelihoods: "Awkward engagements" at the world cultural heritage listing in Bali. *International Journal of Heritage Studies*, 23(9), pp. 846–859.

Marcotte, P. and Bourdeau, L. (2006). Tourists' knowledge of the UNESCO designation of World Heritage sites: The case of visitors to Quebec City. *International Journal of Arts Management*, 8(2), pp. 4–13.

Marques, C., Reis, E. and Menezes, J. (2010). Profiling the segments of visitors to Portuguese protected areas. *Journal of Sustainable Tourism*, 18(8), pp. 971–996.

Marzeion, B. and Levermann, A. (2014). Loss of cultural World Heritage and currently inhabited places to sea-level rise. *Environmental Research Letters*, 9(3), pp. 1–7.

Mason, R.J. (2015). Preservation and preemption in Japan's Shirakami Sanchi World Heritage area. *Management of Environmental Quality: An International Journal*, 26(3), pp. 448–465.

McGuiness, V., Rodger, K., Pearce, J., Newsome, D. and Eagles, P.F.J. (2017). Short-stop visitation in Shark Bay World Heritage area: An importance-performance analysis. *Journal of Ecotourism*, 16(1), pp. 24–40.

McIntosh, A.J. and Prentice, R.C. (1999). Affirming authenticity: Consuming cultural heritage. *Annals of Tourism Research*, 26(3), pp. 589–612.

McKercher, B. (2002). Towards a classification of cultural tourists. *International Journal of Tourism Research*, 4, pp. 29–38.

McKercher, B. and du Cros, H. (2003). Testing a cultural tourism typology. *International Journal of Tourism Research*, 5(1), pp. 45–58.

Meric, H.J. and Hunt, J. (1998). Ecotourists' motivational and demographic characteristics: A case of North Carolina travelers. *Journal of Travel Research*, 26(4), pp. 57–61.

Meskell, L. (2013). UNESCO's World Heritage Convention at 40: Challenging the economic and political order of international heritage conservation. *Current Anthropology*, 54(4), pp. 483–494.

Meskell, L. (2015). Transacting UNESCO World Heritage: Gifts and exchanges on a global scale. *Social Anthropology*, 23(1), pp. 3–21.

Meskell, L. and Brumann, C. (2015). UNESCO and new world orders. In L. Meskell (Ed.), *Global Heritage: A Reader* (pp. 22–42). Chichester, UK: John Wiley & Sons, Inc.

Meskell, L., Liuzza, C., Bertacchini, E. and Saccone, D. (2015). Multilateralism and UNESCO World Heritage: Decision-making, states parties and political processes. *International Journal of Heritage Studies*, 21(5), pp. 423–440.

Millar, S. (2006). Stakeholders and community participation. In A. Leask and A. Fyall (Eds.), *Managing World Heritage Sites* (pp. 37–54). Oxford: Butterworth-Heinemann.

Milman, A. (2015). Preserving the cultural identity of a World Heritage site: The impact of Chichen Itza's souvenir vendors. *International Journal of Culture, Tourism and Hospitality Research*, 9(3), pp. 241–260.

Milman, A. and Pizam, A. (1995). The role of awareness and familiarity with a destination: The central Florida case. *Journal of Travel Research*, 33(3), pp. 21–27.

Ministry of Tourism and Civil Aviation (2012). *National Sustainable Tourism Masterplan for Belize 2030*. Available at: http://cdn.gov.bz/tourism/National%20Sustainable%20Tourism%20Master%20Plan.pdf. [Accessed on 25 February 2019].

Miura, K. and Sarjana, I.M. (2016). The World Heritage nomination of Balinese cultural landscapes: Local struggles and expectations. In V.T. King (Ed.), *UNESCO in Southeast Asia: World Heritage Sites in Comparative Perspective* (pp. 274–290). Copenhagen: NIAS.

Morgan, N. and Pritchard, A. (2000). *Advertising in Tourism and Leisure*. Oxford: Butterworth-Heinemann.

Morgan, N. and Pritchard, A. (2014). Key issues in destination brand management. In S. McCabe (Ed.), *The Routledge Handbook of Tourism Marketing* (pp. 411–424). London: Routledge.

Moscardo, G., Green, D. and Greenwood, T. (2001). How great is the Great Barrier Reef! Tourists' knowledge and understanding of the World Heritage status of the Great Barrier Reef. *Tourism Recreation Research*, 26(1), pp. 19–25.

Musitelli, J. (2002). World Heritage, between universalism and globalization. *International Journal of Cultural Property*, 11(2), pp. 323–336.

National Institute of Urban Affairs (2015). *Urban heritage in Indian cities*. National Institute of Urban Affairs. New Delhi, India.

National Park Service (n.d.). *Recreation Visitors by Month: Yellowstone NP*. Available at: https://irma.nps.gov/Stats/SSRSReports/Park%20Specific%20Reports/Recreation%20Visitors%20By%20Month%20(1979%20-%20Last%20Calendar%20Year)?Park=YELL. [Accessed on 25 February 2019].

National Park Service (2017). *Yellowstone National Park Visitor Use Study: Summer, 2016*. U.S. Department of the Interior.

Ng, S.I., Lee, J.A. and Soutar, G.N. (2007). Tourists' intention to visit a country: The impact of cultural distance. *Tourism Management*, 28, pp. 1497–1506.

Nguyen, T.H.H. and Cheung, C. (2014). The classification of heritage tourists: A case of Hue city, Vietnam. *Journal of Heritage Tourism*, 9(1), pp. 35–50.

OECD (2009). *The Impact of Culture on Tourism*. Paris: OECD Publishing.

Palau-Saumell, R., Forgas-Coll, S., Sánchez-García, J. and Prats-Planagumà, L. (2012). Tourist behavior intentions and the moderator effect of knowledge of UNESCO World Heritage sites: The case of La Sagrada Família. *Journal of Travel Research*, 52(3), pp. 364–376.

Parnwell, M.J.G. (2016). Heritage management and tourism development in Hoi An, Vietnam. In V.T. King (Ed.), *UNESCO in Southeast Asia: World Heritage Sites in Comparative Perspective* (pp. 75–107). Copenhagen: NIAS.

Patuelli, R., Mussoni, M. and Candela, G. (2013). The effects of World Heritage sites on domestic tourism: A spatial interaction model for Italy. *Journal of Geographical Systems*, 15(3), pp. 369–402.

Pechlaner, H. and Volgger, M. (2013). Towards a comprehensive view of tourism governance: Relationships between the corporate governance of tourism service firms and territorial governance. *International Journal of Globalisation and Small Business*, 5(1–2), pp. 3–19.

Perry, J. (2011). World Heritage hot spots: A global model identifies the 16 natural heritage properties on the World Heritage list most at risk from climate change. *International Journal of Heritage Studies*, 17(5), pp. 426–441.

Piggott-McKellar, A.E. and McNamara, K.E. (2017). Last chance tourism and the Great Barrier Reef. *Journal of Sustainable Tourism*, 25(3), pp. 397–415.

Plets, G. (2015). Ethno-nationalism, asymmetric federalism and Soviet perceptions of the past: (World) heritage activism in the Russian federation. *Journal of Social Archaeology*, 15(1), pp. 67–93.

Plog, S. (1974). Why destination areas rise and fall in popularity. *Cornell Hotel and Restaurant Administration Quarterly*, 14(4), pp. 55–58.

Plog, S. (2001). Why destination areas rise and fall in popularity: An update of a *Cornell Quarterly* classic. *Cornell Hotel and Restaurant Administration Quarterly*, 42(3), pp. 13–24.

Poria, Y., Butler, R. and Airey, D. (2003). The core of heritage tourism. *Annals of Tourism Research*, 30(1), pp. 238–254.

Poria, Y., Reichel, A. and Biran, A. (2006). Heritage site perceptions and motivations to visit. *Journal of Travel Research*, 44(3), pp. 318–326.

Poria, Y., Reichel, A. and Cohen, R. (2011). World Heritage site: An effective brand for an archaeological site? *Journal of Heritage Tourism*, 6(3), pp. 197–208.

Poria, Y., Reichel, A. and Cohen, R. (2013). Tourists perceptions of World Heritage site and its designation. *Tourism Management*, 35, pp. 272–274.

Prideaux, B. and Thompson, M. (2017). Impact of climate change on tourism in World Heritage sites: A case study from the wet tropics region of Australia. In J.S. Chen and N.K. Prebensen (Eds.), *Nature Tourism* (pp. 82–94). London: Routledge.

Rakic, T. and Chambers, D. (2007). World Heritage: Exploring the tension between the national and the "universal." *Journal of Heritage Tourism*, 2(3), pp. 145–155.

Rasoolimanesh, S.M., Jaafar, M., Ahmad, A.G. and Barghi, R. (2017). Community participation in World Heritage site conservation and tourism development. *Tourism Management*, 58, pp. 142–153.

Rasoolimanesh, S.M., Ringle, C.M., Jaafar, M. and Ramayah, T. (2017). Urban vs. rural destinations: Residents' perceptions, community participation and support for tourism development. *Tourism Management*, 60, pp. 147–158.

Rasoolimanesh, S.M., Roldán, J.L., Jaafar, M. and Ramayah, T. (2017). Factors influencing residents' perceptions toward tourism development: Differences across rural and urban World Heritage sites. *Journal of Travel Research*, 56(6), pp. 760–775.

Reed, A. (2015). The social life of the castles: Inclusion, exclusion, and heritage sites in Ghana. In L. Bourdeau, M. Gravari-Barbas, and M. Robinson (Eds.), *World Heritage, Tourism and Identity: Inscription and Co-Production* (pp. 147–156). Burlington, VT: Ashgate Publishing Company.

Remoaldo, P.C., Vareiro, L., Ribeiro, J.C. and Santos, J.F. (2014). Does gender affect visiting a World Heritage site? *Visitor Studies*, 17(1), pp. 89–106.

Ribaudo, G. and Figini, P. (2017). The puzzle of tourism demand at destinations hosting UNESCO World Heritage sites: An analysis of tourism flows for Italy. *Journal of Travel Research*, 56(4), pp. 521–542.

Richards, G. (2007). *ATLAS Cultural Tourism Survey: Summary Report 2007*. Available at: www.tram-research.com/atlas/ATLAS%20Cultural%20Tourism%20 Survey%202007.PDF. [Accessed on 18 January 2019].

Ripp, M. and Rodwell, D. (2017). Governance in UNESCO World Heritage sites: Reframing the role of management plans as a tool to improve community engagement. In S. Makuvaza (Ed.), *Aspects of Management Planning for Cultural World Heritage Sites: Principles, Approaches and Practices* (pp. 241–253). Cham, Switzerland: Springer.

Rodwell, D. (2002). The World Heritage Convention and the exemplary management of complex sites. *Journal of Architectural Conservation*, 8(3), pp. 40–60.

Rogerson, C.M. and van der Merwe, C.D. (2016). Heritage tourism in the global South: Development impacts of the cradle of humankind World Heritage site, South Africa. *Local Economy*, 31(1–2), pp. 234–248.

Ryan, J. and Silvanto, S. (2011). A brand for all the nations: The development of the World Heritage brand in emerging markets. *Marketing Intelligence & Planning*, 29(3), pp. 305–318.

Ryan, J. and Silvanto, S. (2014). A study of the key strategic drivers of the use of the World Heritage site designation as a destination brand. *Journal of Travel & Tourism Marketing*, 31(3), pp. 327–343.

Salazar, N.B. (2014). 1972–2012: Forty years of World Heritage Convention: Time to take tourism seriously? In M. Gravari-Barbas and S. Jacquot (Eds.), *Patrimoine Mondial et Développement au Défi du Tourisme Durable* (pp. 27–45). Québec, Canada: Presses de l'Université du Québec.

Salazar, N.B. (2015). The local-to-global dynamics of World Heritage interpretation. In L. Bourdeau, M. Gravari-Barbas, and M. Robinson (Eds.), *World Heritage, Tourism and Identity: Inscription and Co-Production* (pp. 121–130). Burlington, VT: Ashgate Publishing Company.

Schmitt, T.M. (2009). Global cultural governance: Decision-making concerning World Heritage between politics and science. *Erdkunde*, 63(2), pp. 103–121.

Schmutz, V. and Elliott, M.A. (2017). World Heritage and the scientific consecration of "outstanding universal value." *International Journal of Comparative Sociology*, 58(2), pp. 140–159.

Shackley, M. (2005). Managing the cedars of Lebanon: Botanical gardens or living forests? In D. Harrison and M. Hitchcock (Eds.), *The Politics of World Heritage: Negotiating Tourism and Conservation* (pp. 137–145). Clevedon, UK: Channel View.

Shackley, M. (2006). Visitor management at World Heritage sites. In A. Leask and A. Fyall (Eds.), *Managing World Heritage Sites* (pp. 83–93). Oxford: Butterworth-Heinemann.

Singh, J.P. (2011). *United Nations Educational, Scientific and Cultural Organization (UNESCO): Creating Norms for a Complex World*. London: Routledge.

Smith, M. (2002). A critical evaluation of the global accolade: The significance of World Heritage site status for maritime greenwich. *International Journal of Heritage Studies*, 8(2), pp. 137–151.

Stebbins, R.A. (1996). Cultural tourism as serious leisure. *Annals of Tourism Research*, 23(4), pp. 948–950.

Stoddard, J.E., Evans, M.R. and Davé, D.S. (2008). Sustainable tourism: The case of the Blue Ridge National Heritage area. *Cornell Hospitality Quarterly*, 49(3), pp. 245–257.

Strasser, P. (2002). "Putting reform into action": Thirty years of the World Heritage Convention: How to reform a convention without changing its regulations. *International Journal of Cultural Property*, 11(2), pp. 215–266.

Strategic Planning Division, Tourism New South Wales. (1995). *New South Wales Government Submission to the HORSCERA Inquiry into World Heritage*. p. 1.

Su, M.M. and Wall, G. (2012). Global-local relationships and governance issues at the Great Wall World Heritage site, China. *Journal of Sustainable Tourism*, 20(8), pp. 1067–1086.

Su, M.M. and Wall, G. (2015). Community involvement at Great Wall World Heritage sites, Beijing, China. *Current Issues in Tourism*, 18(2), pp. 137–157.

Su, M.M. and Wall, G. (2016). A comparison of tourists' and residents' uses of Temple of Heaven World Heritage site, China. *Asia Pacific Journal of Tourism Research*, 21(8), pp. 905–930.

Su, M.M., Wall, G. and Liu, K. (2016). Heritâge tourism and livelihood sustainability of a resettled rural community: Mount Sanqingshan World Heritage site, China. *Journal of Sustainable Tourism*, 24(5), pp. 735–757.

Su, Y.-W. and Lin, H.-L. (2014). Analysis of international tourist arrivals worldwide: The role of World Heritage sites. *Tourism Management*, 40, pp. 46–58.

Sun, J., Zhou, Y. and Wang, X. (2017). Place construction in the context of World Heritage tourism: The case of "Kaiping Diaolou and Villages." *Journal of Tourism and Cultural Change*, pp. 1–17. https://doi.org/10.1080/14766825.2017.1395441

Theuma, N. and Grima, R. (2006). The megalithic temples of malta: Towards a re-evaluation of heritage. In A. Leask and A. Fyall (Eds.), *Managing World Heritage Sites* (pp. 264–272). Oxford: Butterworth-Heinemann.

Thompson, J. (2007, September 13–15). Engagement in public-private partnership in cultural heritage: The case of Herculaneum, Italy. In proceedings of *ICCROM: International Forum on Privatisation and Cultural Heritage*, Catania, Italy.

Timothy, D.J. (1998). Collecting places: Geodetic lines in tourist space. *Journal of Travel & Tourism Marketing*, 7(4), pp. 123–129.

Timothy, D.J. and Nyaupane, G.P. (Eds.). (2009). *Cultural Heritage and Tourism in the Developing World: A Regional Perspective*. London: Routledge.

Tisdell, C. and Wilson, C. (2002). World Heritage listing of Australian natural sites: Tourism stimulus and its economic value. *Economic Analysis & Policy*, 32(2), pp. 27–49.

Turton, S.M. (2005). Managing environmental impacts of recreation and tourism in rainforests of the Wet Tropics of Queensland World Heritage area. *Geographical Research*, 43(2), pp. 140–151.

UNESCO (n.d.-a). *Lake Malawi National Park*. Available at: https://whc.unesco. org/en/list/289. [Accessed on 25 October 2018].

UNESCO (n.d.-b). *Sustainable Tourism*. Available at: https://whc.unesco.org/en/ tourism/. [Accessed on 30 October 2018].

UNESCO (n.d.-c). *World Heritage List*. Available at: http://whc.unesco.org/en/list/. [Accessed on 21 February 2019].

UNESCO (n.d.-d). *Yellowstone National Park*. Available at: https://whc.unesco.org/ en/list/28/. [Accessed on 28 February 2019].

UNESCO (1972). *Convention Concerning the Protection of the World Cultural and Natural Heritage*. Available at: http://whc.unesco.org/archive/convention-en.pdf. [Accessed on 22 January 2019].

UNESCO (2008). *World Heritage Information Kit*. Paris: UNESCO.

UNESCO (2009). *State of Conservation: Belize Barrier Reef System (Belize)*. Available at: https://whc.unesco.org/en/soc/743. [Accessed on 25 February 2019].

UNESCO (2010). *Decision: 34 COM 5F.2: Report on the World Heritage Thematic Programmes*. Available at: https://whc.unesco.org/en/decisions/4240. [Accessed on 24 February 2019].

UNESCO (2013). *Decisions Adopted by the World Heritage Committee at Its 37th Session (Phnom Penh, 2013)*. Paris: UNESCO.

UNESCO (2015). *Policy Document for the Integration of a Sustainable Development Perspective into the Processes of the World Heritage Convention*. Paris: UNESCO. Available at: https://whc.unesco.org/en/sustainabledevelopment/. [Accessed on 22 October 2018].

UNESCO (2017). *Operational Guidelines for the Implementation of the World Heritage Convention*. Paris: UNESCO.

UNESCO (2018a). *State of Conservation: Belize Barrier Reef System (Belize)*. Available at: https://whc.unesco.org/en/soc/3807. [Accessed on 25 February 2019].

UNESCO (2018b). *State of Conservation of Lake Malawi World Heritage Site*. Available at: https://whc.unesco.org/document/167399. [Accessed on 25 February 2019].

Urry, J. (2002). *The Tourist Gaze* (2nd ed.). London: Sage Publications Ltd.

Valderrama, F. (1995). *A History of UNESCO*. Paris: UNESCO.

VanBlarcom, B.L. and Kayahan, C. (2011). Assessing the economic impact of a UNESCO World Heritage designation. *Journal of Heritage Tourism*, 6(2), pp. 143–164.

Van der Aa, B.J.M. (2005). *Preserving the Heritage of Humanity? Obtaining World Heritage Status and the Impacts of Listing*. Unpublished Dissertation. Ph.D. in Physical Sciences, University of Groningen, Groningen, Netherlands.

Van der Aa, B.J.M., Groote, P.D. and Huigen, P.P.P. (2005). World Heritage as NIMBY? The case of the Dutch part of the Wadden Sea. In D. Harrison and M. Hitchcock (Eds.), *The Oolitics of World Heritage: Negotiating Tourism and Conservation* (pp. 11–22). Clevedon, UK: Channel View Publications.

Vella, C., Bocancea, E., Urban, T.M., Knodell, A.R., Tuttle, C.A. and Alcock, S.E. (2015). Looting and vandalism around a World Heritage site: Documenting modern damage to archaeological heritage in Petra's hinterland. *Journal of Field Archaeology*, 40(2), pp. 221–235.

Vong, F. (2016). Application of cultural tourist typology in a gaming destination: Macao. *Current Issues in Tourism*, 19(9), pp. 949–965.

Vong, L.T.-N. (2015). The mediating role of place identity in the relationship between residents' perceptions of heritage tourism and place attachment: The Macau youth experience. *Journal of Heritage Tourism*, 10(4), pp. 344–356.

Vrdoljak, A.F. (2008). Article 13: World Heritage Committee and international assistance. In F. Francioni (Ed.), *The 1972 World Heritage Convention: A Commentary* (pp. 219–241). Oxford: Oxford University Press.

Wardell-Johnson, G., Schoeman, D., Schlacher, T., Wardell-Johnson, A., Weston, M.A., Shimizu, Y. and Conroy, G. (2015). Re-framing values for World Heritage future: What type of icon will K'gari-Fraser Island become? *Australasian Journal of Environmental Management*, 22(2), pp. 124–148.

Weaver, D.B. and Lawton, L.J. (2002). Overnight ecotourist market segmentation in the Gold Coast hinterland of Australia. *Journal of Travel Research*, 40, pp. 270–280.

Willems, W.J.H. (2014). The future of World Heritage and the emergence of transnational heritage regimes. *Heritage & Society*, 7(2), pp. 105–120.

Williams, K. (2004). The meanings and effectiveness of World Heritage designations in the USA. *Current Issues in Tourism*, 7(4), pp. 412–416.

Winter, T. (2005). Landscape, memory and heritage: New year celebrations at Angkor, Cambodia. In D. Harrison and M. Hitchcock (Eds.), *The Politics of World Heritage: Negotiating Tourism and Conservation* (pp. 50–65). Clevedon, UK: Channel View.

Woosnam, K.M., Aleshinloye, K.D., Ribeiro, M.A., Stylidis, D., Jiang, J. and Erul, E. (2018). Social determinants of place attachment at a World Heritage site. *Tourism Management*, 67, pp. 139–146.

Wuepper, D. (2017). What is the value of World Heritage status for a German national park? A choice experiment from Jasmund, 1 year after inscription. *Tourism Economics*, 23(5), pp. 1114–1123.

Xiang, Y. and Wall, G. (2015). Implications of World Heritage designation for local residents: A case study from Taishan and Taiqian, China. In L. Bourdeau, M. Gravari-Barbas, and M. Robinson (Eds.), *World Heritage, Tourism and Identity: Inscription and Co-Production* (pp. 51–68). Burlington, VT: Ashgate Publishing Company.

Yan, C. and Morrison, A.M. (2008). The influence of visitors' awareness of World Heritage listings: A case study of Huangshan, Xidi, and Hongcun in Southern Anhui, China. *Journal of Heritage Tourism*, 2(3), pp. 184–195.

Yan, H. (2015). World Heritage as discourse: Knowledge, discipline and dissonance in Fujian Tulou sites. *International Journal of Heritage Studies*, 21(1), pp. 65–80.

Yang, C.-H., Lin, H.-L. and Han, C.-C. (2010). Analysis of international tourist arrivals in China: The role of World Heritage sites. *Tourism Management*, 31, pp. 827–837.

Yang, C.-H. and Lin, H.-Y. (2014). Revisiting the relationship between World Heritage sites and tourism. *Tourism Economics*, 20(1), pp. 73–86.

Yang, Y., Xue, L. and Jones, T.E. (2019). Tourism-enhancing effect of World Heritage sites: Panacea or placebo? A meta-analysis. *Annals of Tourism Research*, 75, pp. 29–41.

Yau, M.K.-S., McKercher, B. and Packer, T.L. (2004). Traveling with a disability: More than just an access issue. *Annals of Tourism Research*, 31(4), pp. 946–960.

Zacharias, D. (2008). The UNESCO regime for the protection of World Heritage as prototype of an autonomy-gaining international institution. *German Law Journal*, 9(11), pp. 1833–1864.

Zhang, R. (2017). World Heritage listing and changes of political values: A case study in West Lake cultural landscape in Hongzhou, China. *International Journal of Heritage Studies*, 23(3), pp. 215–233.

Index

Printed in the United States
by Baker & Taylor Publisher Services